Does Your Financial Plan Create Wealth?

Are You Sure?

This Book Will ROCK Your World

CREATE WEALTH ON AUTO-PILOT

Unlock Your Treasure Chest!

Here Are Your Keys to Becoming a Millionaire

By Raleigh Makarechian
& Gerald R. Gallegos

ISBN: 978-0-6151-5977-5

Contents

Preface 4
Objective 6
Authors' Background
  Raleigh Makarechian 7
  Gerald (Jerry) R. Gallegos 8
Defining Your Goals 9
The Great American Dream 10
The Financial Rules Have Changed 11
The Unfortunate Facts of Life 13
The Ticking Tax Bomb 15
Interest Expenses 22
Your Secret Weapon for Creating Wealth 23
The Power of Arbitrage 29
The Most Overlooked Investment Tool 31
Becoming Your Own Banker 44
The Stock Market and Mutual Funds 47
High Yield Investments 51
Opportunity Costs 55
The Power of Leverage 57
Summary 62
Appendix 65
Case Study – Actual Client Plan 66
  The Johnson Family – The Rest of Their Story 72
  Building <u>Your</u> Plan – A Guide for You 77
  Summary of Services Offered 83
Glossary 84
References and Acknowledgements 87
Quotes 89

PREFACE

Millions of Americans are facing a major financial crisis in **their** lives. The disturbing aspect about this statement is that many of them don't even realize what is happening.

So what is this major impending crisis? By the way, if you don't believe us, stop and take a moment to think about what we are saying. The truth about this statement is quite evident!

Ask yourself, how many people, you know, who…

- Are living from pay check to pay check?
- Are up to their eye balls in credit card debt?
- Have no money saved for an unforeseen financial emergency?
- Have no money to take a family vacation?
- Have no money to buy a new car?
- Have no clue how they are going to pay for their children's college education?
- Are totally unprepared for retirement?

This is not a joke! People are being led down the wrong path and it is time to stop and listen to the truth.

DO WE HAVE YOUR ATTENTION YET?

Before we begin, stop for a second! **Relax - and dare to dream**!

What kind of a difference would it make in your life if you earned an extra $500 dollars per month? What about an extra $1,000 each month? Let's get really bold and think about an extra $5,000 per month or $100,000 per year. Think about the possibilities of taking your dream vacation, buying that new car, not worrying about paying your bills!

If you can dream and you are willing to work in a much smarter way, you can achieve your dreams. That is what this book is all about! It was written with three specific goals in mind.

1. To help anyone get out of debt and become financially independent.

2. To assist successful investors in protecting their hard earned money.

3. To guide individuals in transferring their wealth tax-free to future generations.

If you are one of the fortunate few who have already achieved financial success, we congratulate you! Parts of this book may be redundant; however, if you take the time to read all of it, you will understand how this book pertains to the future financial welfare of your children and grandchildren.

Let us be very honest with you! This book is not one of those books written for the sole purpose of making you feel good. It was written to get your interest and attention and to be your common sense guide to financial prosperity. Why? Because the concepts in this book work!

Have you ever thought there must be something wrong with the financial strategies taught by many, so-called, financial experts? Could it be they are not at all interested in **your** financial well being, but only in theirs? Could it be, much of the information they are teaching you about saving for your children's college education, a home or retirement is entirely wrong? If you answered yes to any of these questions, then this book is for you!

As stated before, it is important to realize that many honest, hard working, middle class families in our country are facing a future financial crisis. They must be willing to step up to the plate and take responsibility for their financial well being and most of all they must "Stop the insanity of following investment strategies that do not work."

In spite of this gloomy outlook, there is good news! We understand your pain! We know there is a better way! This book introduces concepts which, before now, you may have not ever seen. It will be your guide to achieving financial success, if you will discipline yourself and commit to learning and applying the concepts. These concepts have worked for thousands of families in the past and they have been implemented by the very wealthy for over a century; they can work just as easily for you.

Note: This book is not about get-rich-quick schemes. The information in this book outlines a specific strategy. Learn and apply the concepts in your life so that you will be able to meet or exceed your financial goals in the near future. Enjoy the benefits. You deserve it!

People who are concerned about their health continually work out to stay physically fit. Many of them belong to health clubs. Those who really want to go to the next level in fitness often times pay to have a personal trainer or health coach. This book is your guide and we intend for it to become your financial wellness coach. Welcome to the next level of financial fitness!

OBJECTIVE OF THIS BOOK

"Insanity is doing the same thing over and over again and expecting different results!"

You have the ability to reinvent yourself and completely **change** your financial life in five years or less. With the correct information, would you decide to make that change? (A high school graduate goes to college and accomplishes this in four years; most trade schools are structured with a curriculum of one - two years.) The point is-- a positive change is possible when you make that decision! Do not lose sight of this goal as you read this book.

Let's talk about wealth for a moment. What does it mean to you? Is it having a bigger house, a new car or paying for your children's education? Maybe it is, knowing you have enough money to pay next month's bills. The fact is wealth is different for everyone! So, how do you attain it?

The goal of writing this book is to provide you with the information necessary for you to begin a journey to reach your financial goals. Each chapter describes a separate principle which you will need to develop your short-term and long-term plan. Please don't skip ahead. Remember, this book is about creating wealth!

If you purchased this book to help you make a change in your life, we have the responsibility to make sure we deliver. However, in order for you to succeed, **you have the responsibility to take action.** Not next year, but today!

THE BEGINNING – This is not an option! Before you continue, we are going to insist that you agree to three specific action items. On a daily basis, you must begin to:

- REMOVE PROCRASTINATION FROM YOUR LIFE
- DEVELOP A HABIT TO THINK OUTSIDE THE BOX
- BEGIN A REGIMEN OF CONTINUING EDUCATION

Why is this essential? This book is not just about strategies, it is about **action**! Within the next five years there will be individuals who read this book and become self-made millionaires. The decision is up to you! Our goal is for you to be one of them.

Let's get started. Let us help you to begin the process outlined in the three action items.

Remove procrastination – Read this book within the next 7 days! Think outside the box and challenge your thinking - What is the highest annualized percentage rate of return **you** can earn on a five thousand dollar investment? Is it 5%, 10%, 300% or more? The answer is, **all the above** and **we will prove it!** Continuing education – within 60 days, read at least 3 books, listed in the references section of this book.

Raleigh Makarechian

I'll bet you are wondering how I came to be a speaker and a financial liberator! Why should you listen to me? That is a great question and I am excited to share the origin of my story.

My name is Raleigh Makarechian. I obtained a Bachelor of Science degree in Accounting from the University of Michigan. I am an Alternative Investment Specialist with Wealth2020, Inc. My job is to show people how to establish their own Banking System and how to double or triple their retirement nest egg, with little or no additional money out of pocket.

While I have been in Business and Financial planning for over twelve years, it is really the last five years that are going to define my success. I spent much of the last five years Day Trading the Stock Market, Investing in Real Estate and looking for what most would call "The Holy Grail" of investment returns. Why would I do that? I want to "Retire Early and Retire Wealthy!" You see, I don't want to wait till age 65 to see if my financial planning was more than adequate. I want to be in the driver's seat long before that!

As you probably know, Real Estate investing is hard work and without proper guidance it can be risky; the same goes for Day Trading the markets. While I made a lot of money at both, I was still very reluctant to put all of my investment funds into one or both of these vehicles at once. Not to mention the fact that I was looking for a way for my friends and family to increase their wealth with no risk to their hard earned money. Accordingly, I started looking for better ways to invest. I set forth a few simple criteria in my search:

1. I did not want to lose principal, ever!
2. I did not want to spend day and night working towards this goal.
3. I wanted to double my money every 3 to 4 years…like clockwork.
4. I wanted predictability in my investing.

I went to numerous seminars, read many books, interviewed some of the best financial planners I could locate and spent countless hours on the internet looking for a solution.

Well, the great news is….**I FOUND IT!**

Gerald R. Gallegos

My name is Gerald R. Gallegos (Jerry). My formal education includes obtaining a Civil Engineering degree from the University of Denver. Since graduating from college I gained valuable experience and perspective as a business owner and sales manager with a leading, Fortune 500 Corporation. My experiences as an entrepreneur have contributed to developing many of the concepts presented in this book.

I love working with positive, like-minded people. My true passion for business success is investing in real estate and mentoring others who have common goals to establish a sound financial portfolio that includes profitable real estate transactions.

As a small business owner I quickly learned that creating your own job is not necessarily synonymous with creating wealth. For that reason, I changed paths and decided to dedicate my time and efforts to researching and learning about investment strategies that would, in fact, lead to the creation of wealth.

Throughout my career as a real estate investor, I have perfected and implemented a process that allows investors to purchase properties with little or no money down. I especially enjoy transactions that involve purchasing or selling properties by utilizing a strategy of lease/option contracts. It is gratifying to see the long-term results, of a properly structured lease/option contract. This type of sales transaction can provide substantial benefits to the seller and tenant/buyer.

Co-authoring this book allows me to share many of my experiences as an entrepreneur and to teach others how to avoid some of the mistakes that I made along the way.

On a personal note, I am a person who believes that nothing in life ever happens by chance! Raleigh and I met at a monthly meeting of a local real estate investment group. After numerous meetings and careful consideration, we determined that our interests, in helping others to succeed were mutual.

Raleigh Makarechian's extensive background in the financial services industry and my background as a full time real estate investor presented a unique opportunity. It has guided us toward establishing a relationship that allows us to attain our common goals of helping other people to succeed. The fact that Raleigh is also a seasoned real estate investor, made for an even better business relationship.

In order to achieve our goal of reaching the masses, we decided to write "Creating Wealth on Auto-Pilot" and to market it via the internet. It is our solemn belief the information within this book will make a positive and profound difference in the lives of many people who are willing to learn about and follow a <u>proven</u> system. We call this <u>The Financial Wellness System</u>™.

By the way! Continuing education is a daily routine for us. Welcome to the team.

DEFINING YOUR GOALS

Daily, we are bombarded with television infomercials that tell us how Jane, Jack, Mary or Bob were totally broke. Miraculously, they took actions that helped them to achieve their life long dreams in a matter of a few short years.

As you watch, you ask yourself, is this really possible? Could anything like this ever happen to me? The successful people in these infomercials would tell you that the defining moment, in their lives was finding the correct vehicle and taking action. The concepts we present in this book can do the same for you.

In order for this book to be of value, you must be willing to change and to accept ideas that are new to you. Most importantly, you must sit down and define **your** goals, not someone else's goals! You already took the first step and your very first goal can be as simple as reading this book within the next week.

The magic of following a proven system is invaluable. We stated that this book is not about getting rich, quick. It is, however, about making a positive change to your financial well-being within the next three to five years. If the financial strategies you have been shown in the past are not meeting your particular goals, then what do you have to lose? We ask you, "What led you to purchase this book, is it because you are not satisfied with your progress to date?"

Caution! Over the years we have consulted with many individual families who were open to new ideas and wanted to make a change in their lives. They made the fatal decision to consult with a friend, family member or financial advisor who either knew nothing about these concepts or did not understand them. **Don't let this happen to you!**

Remember; these concepts have been used for over a century. All you need to do is read the book, write down your goals and follow your plan! You will succeed if you implement the system in your life!

THE GREAT AMERICAN DREAM

The concepts taught in the "Financial Wellness System™" are structured upon understanding the four deadliest wealth creation obstacles! Memorize them, be constantly aware of them and completely eliminate their negative aspects as you strategically develop your future financial plan. They are as follows:

- TAXES
- DEBT
- INFLATION
- PROCRASTINATION

Let's look back in time to understand exactly why many of today's financial plans are simply outdated and not effective in achieving your financial goals.

History tells us that the 'Baby Boomer Generation,' beginning in the mid 1940's, has had a more profound impact on the overall economy than of any other generation in history. The parents of the Baby Boomers experienced the days of the 'Great Depression' and were determined not to let their adversities repeat in the lifetimes of their children. They understood hard work, family values and were committed to achieving The Great American Dream. In those days, they knew, by applying some basic concepts, their children could live that dream. And so it was; a new era was born.

The concepts were as follows…

- GO TO COLLEGE
- GET A GOOD JOB
- BUY A HOUSE
- PAY OFF THE MORTGAGE AS SOON AS POSSIBLE
- SAVE A LITTLE EACH MONTH

You will be set for life! This was actually ROCK SOLID ADVICE because our parents and grandparents…

- LIVED IN THE SAME HOUSE FOR LIFE
- HAD ONE JOB THEIR ENTIRE LIFE
- LIVED ON ONE INCOME
- RETIRED WITH A PENSION
- HAD NO CREDIT CARD DEBT
- SAVED A LITTLE MONEY CONSISTENTLY
- COULD COUNT ON SOCIAL SECURITY

Please understand that our parents and grandparents only needed to conserve their wealth to ensure a successful retirement.

THE FINANCIAL RULES HAVE CHANGED

As we further examine the changing financial rules, I (Jerry) am reminded of a personal experience, a few years back. It made me realize how important it was to use common sense and stop following the crowd.

My wife and I were driving from a small town, in Southern Colorado, to Albuquerque, New Mexico. This route was quite familiar since I had traveled it many times. About ten miles before passing through a small town, we encountered a detour sign. It pointed us in a direction that made no sense to me. However, after watching all the other vehicles go in the direction of the detour, I turned and decided to follow. Besides, they couldn't all be mistaken and headed in the wrong direction. Although, it soon became evident, something was wrong. The detour led to a dead end. It seems someone had put up the detour sign as a joke and caused everyone a considerable delay.

So, what does this story have to do with this book? While studying these concepts you will come to realize someone created a detour in the path of **your** financial prosperity. You will need to apply common sense, stop following outdated financial strategies and get back onto the right road to financial prosperity; if you want to create wealth in your life.

There was a time when all the financial rules began to change. In 1974, a law was enacted that would change the way retirement funds were handled. ERISA, which stands for Employee Retirement Income Security Act was the Act that made 401(k)'s possible. It was passed to help protect employees' retirement money from abuse by their business owners. It was not uncommon to see under-funded pension plans, in blue-chip companies, which created problems for retirees. Where pension plans were funded properly, the plans were worth more than the company itself, so in corporate takeovers, the acquiring company would blatantly dip into funds set aside for future retirees. The 401(k) plans were implemented so that employees would have some control over their financial futures and not be subjected to abuses.

Additionally, these 401(k) plans were a benefit to companies that would otherwise have had to implement a regular pension plan. Not only were the companies no longer entirely responsible for employee pensions, but they also received attractive tax benefits if they chose to match employee contributions. If an employee did not contribute to their 401(k) plan, then the employer had nothing to match; thus providing additional savings. These plans were extremely beneficial to corporate America's bottom line.

Consequently, with no warning, the burden for retirement planning was quietly handed off to the employee. As a result, the employee became responsible for his/her financial future with no training whatsoever. The extent of their education can be summarized as: "Diversify your investments and plan to hold for the long-term." This is hardly a formula for retirement planning success. Unfortunately, the change in the law that was meant to protect employees, turned out to be far more beneficial to the companies for which they worked.

Until this time, the United States' economy had been fueled for decades by the overall ramifications of the Industrial Revolution. A new era was emerging that would have a significant affect on the economy of all nations including the United States. It was the beginning stages of the New Global Economy.

The development of the Internet opened communications between countries like no other technological advancement before. It is responsible for ushering in the Information Technology era which allowed many businesses to expand globally. As a result, our national economy, on many levels, became a part of the new global economy. This change to our economic landscape happened within a few decades. Accordingly, the financial rules for creating wealth and saving for retirement also changed. How do these changes affect you?

Let's take a closer look to see how we are all being affected by these changes.

- WE LIVE IN A GLOBAL ECONOMY
- INFLATION IS CONSTANTLY REDUCING OUR PURCHASING POWER
- TAXES ARE EATING UP OUR SPENDABLE INCOME
- CONSUMER DEBT IS AT AN ALL TIME HIGH
- INDIVIDUALS ARE RESPONSIBLE FOR THEIR RETIREMENT

Unlike our grandparents, we need to **grow** our wealth!

Review these five basic points. You will begin to understand the critical aspects of each and how they apply to you. Use this knowledge as you develop a plan that will ensure your financial success.

THE UNFORTUNATE FACTS OF LIFE

A recent publication by "The US Bureau of Labor and Statistics" indicates that the following is a true description of The Unfortunate Facts of Life.

Out of 100 people expected to reach the age of 65…

- 36 will not live to age 65
- 54 will be financially embarrassed
- 5 will still be working
- 4 will be financially secure
- 1 will be wealthy

The United States of America is considered to be the greatest country in the world and proclaimed as the land of opportunity. How is it possible that only five out of one hundred people will be financially secure?

This book is intended to give insight and new hope to individuals who wish to build wealth, using sound investment practices. The information is intended to be uplifting and positive. However, when it comes to sound financial strategies, there is one topic which might not be quite as positive. But, it plays a vital role in everyone's long-term financial planning. We would be negligent if we did not include this topic in our material. Let's address this topic right now!

The above statistical data, "The Unfortunate Facts of Life" shows us only five out of one hundred individuals reaching the age of sixty five will be financially secure. A closer look reveals a fact which most people overlook or just plainly choose to ignore.

Thirty-six individuals who were supposed to reach the age of 65 will not make it. They will either incur a fatal illness or suffer from an accidental death. The majority of people look at this statistic with the thought in mind, "it will never happen to me." This only happens to other people!

I, (Jerry) began my career in the financial services industry in 1983. My introduction into the market place included selling life insurance. This statistic was drilled into my head as part of corporate training. Little, did I realize, how important it would be while talking to individual prospects about the importance of purchasing life insurance.

Within 60 days I acquired my fourth client. He wanted to purchase two life insurance policies to fund a Buy-Sell-Agreement between him and his business partner. At the same time, he decided to purchase separate polices for his wife and himself. At that time, his engineering consulting firm was doing exceptionally well and he realized that his family's lifestyle would suffer adversely if either he or his wife should pass away prematurely. Three months later, his wife was killed in an auto accident. Exactly four months after, he was killed in an airplane crash; both were in their late thirties. The life insurance proceeds did not take away their children's grief, but it did provide for their financial future. In fact, both children attended college and graduated from the Colorado School of Mines.

More recently, in November of 2006, a neighbor in our community was traveling to the grocery store. Somehow she lost control of her vehicle, crossed over into on-coming traffic and collided head-on into another vehicle. She and the driver of the other vehicle were both killed instantly. Our neighbor was only thirty three and the other driver was thirty four.

These examples are horrible-but real. Just take an inventory of people you have met in your lifetime. You will quickly realize this statistic is accurate, and yes, as unfortunate as this might seem, it can happen to you! It is extremely important you keep this in mind as you develop your long-term financial strategy. Later in this book, we will discuss how your plan will include implementing the proper investment grade life insurance product to serve as a strategic tool in attaining your investment goals.

The information contained in this book teaches you how to build a plan that will provide protection for your family, in the event of your untimely death. It also goes into complete detail to show how you can take control of your finances so that you will be one of the fortunate few who achieves financial independence.

THE TICKING TAX BOMB

We list taxes as one of the four deadliest wealth creation obstacles for a good reason. It is essential for you to understand all the affects they will have on the growth of funds in your individual wealth creation and retirement plans. Once you understand these concepts and strategies, you will be able to develop a financial plan which allows you to control and minimize the amount of taxes that erode your retirement savings and portfolio holdings. The most important aspect of this concept is to learn how to grow your funds in a tax-free environment and eventually withdraw the funds completely tax-free!

As company funded pension plans gradually became a thing of the past, employees were introduced to the concept of saving for retirement with financial vehicles such as 401(k) and IRA plans. The idea was to place a predetermined and restricted amount into a tax-deferred financial investment vehicle so that employees could reap the benefits of not paying taxes on those funds until they retired. It seemed to be a great plan, and for the most part, most employees have gone along with the idea.

But what if this idea is wrong? In fact, DEAD WRONG!

Consider the following example. A farmer walked into a seed store one day and asked the merchant for a one hundred pound sack of seeds for planting a crop of corn. The merchant placed the sack of seeds onto the counter and told him the price. He also told the farmer that he had a choice. He could pay taxes right now on the one hundred pound sack of seeds, or he could defer paying taxes until harvest time and pay taxes on the entire harvest of his corn. The farmer began to laugh! "That is the most absurd question I have ever heard. Of course I will pay my taxes now! I am paying on a much smaller amount!"

This seems like very sound advice and pure common sense. So why do we do exactly the opposite when we consider saving for retirement. In a traditional IRA or 401(k), everyone chooses to defer paying taxes on a small amount invested each year and then pay a much larger tax upon withdrawal of the funds at the time of retirement. That is what we have been taught as being the most prudent way to save for retirement.

Traditional thinking, leads us to believe we will all be in a much lower tax bracket at the time of retirement than we are today. If this were true, we would not have much in the form of taxes to pay at the time of retirement. Again, could this information be wrong? Let's take a closer look!

The average family in America will have two wage earners just to keep up with yearly expenses. If there are two children during the prime income years, the family will claim a total of four dependents in order to solve for tax deductions. In addition to claiming dependents as tax deductions, the family will be able to write off a portion of interest expenses for a mortgage on their home. Based upon traditional retirement planning advice, there are two significant factors which will eliminate tax deductions and, consequently, increase the amount of taxes a couple will pay at retirement age.

- They will no longer have the two deductions for their children
- They will lose the mortgage interest expense deduction on their home because it will, in all likely-hood, be paid off.

We find the average family in America is struggling just to make ends meet. You must now ask yourself whether you plan to retire and receive a much lower income or if you prefer to retire with the same or more income so you can enjoy your retirement years. If you wish to retire with more money or maintain the same level of income, you will be shocked when you understand how your retirement plan, using a traditional 401(k) or IRA, is actually structured in favor of Uncle Sam and not you!

Let's use the analogy of the farmer purchasing a sack of seeds and use it as an example of how this concept applies to your 401(k) or IRA.

Is it better to pay taxes on the Seed or the Harvest?

A simple case study reveals the realities of traditional plans!

Did you realize that Uncle Sam plays a tax shell game with our IRA, 401(k) and other Qualified Retirement Plans?

- Seed (We are encouraged to take tax deductions on the Seed.)
  - $6,000 contribution x 33% tax bracket = $2,000 annual tax deduction
  - 35 years of contributions x $2,000 tax deduction = **$70,000 total tax savings**
- Harvest (At Harvest time, we pay dearly for those tiny tax deductions)
  - After 35 years, assume that the plan grows to $1,000,000 @ 7.5%
  - Retiree decides to live on interest of $75,000 ($1,000,000 x 7.5%)
  - Calculate taxes owed: $75,000 x 33% = 25,000 taxes ($50,000 net spend-able income to retiree)
  - **$25,000 tax payments in year 1 of retirement****

****Note: By year 3, the retiree has paid MORE in taxes than he/she saved in deductions over a 35 year period! In ten years this retiree will pay $250,000 in taxes.**

Let's look at another example. We use a traditional IRA with the following assumptions. You will quickly understand how this scenario is creating an event in the future that is comparable to the farmer paying taxes on the harvest and not the sack of seeds!

- Above average tax deductible deposits each year
- Deposits begin at age thirty five

- Deposits end at age sixty four
- Earnings goal is a minimum of nine percent per year
- No loss of principal in any year

In addition to creating a ticking tax bomb, everyone is aware traditional 401(k)'s and IRA's are retirement savings vehicles that have limitations and restrictions.

- An individual is only allowed to contribute a limited tax exempt amount each year
- Loans against the funds restrict the use of the funds
- Severe penalties will be imposed for early withdrawal
- Distribution of funds beginning at age 70 ½ are mandatory
- Funds distributed at time of retirement are **100%** taxable

Chart A, on the following page, depicts the growth of a 401(k) plan with an above average deposit by the Johnson Family beginning at age 35. Over time, at an assumed rate of 9.0% per year and assuming no loss to principal (**not guaranteed with traditional plans**) in any year, the Johnson's accumulate $1,188,602. On the surface, it appears as though the Johnson's are in fine shape.

Chart A:

Johnson Family Contributions to 401K $8,000 per year contributions age 35 to age 64				
Husband/Wife Same Age	**Annual Contribution**	**Cummulative Contributions**	**End of Year Total Earnings Assume 9.0%**	**End of Year New 401K Balance**
Age 35	$8,000	$8,000	$720	$8,720
Age 36	$8,000	$16,000	$1,570	$18,225
Age 37	$8,000	$24,000	$3,221	$28,585
Age 38	$8,000	$32,000	$5,023	$39,878
Age 39	$8,000	$40,000	$6,921	$52,187
Age 40	$8,000	$48,000	$8,920	$65,603
Age 41	$8,000	$56,000	$11,027	$80,228
Age 42	$8,000	$64,000	$13,253	$96,168
Age 43	$8,000	$72,000	$15,608	$113,543
Age 44	$8,000	$80,000	$18,104	$132,482
Age 45	$8,000	$88,000	$20,753	$153,126
Age 46	$8,000	$96,000	$23,569	$175,627
Age 47	$8,000	$104,000	$26,568	$200,154
Age 48	$8,000	$112,000	$29,765	$226,887
Age 49	$8,000	$120,000	$33,179	$256,027
Age 50	$8,000	$128,000	$36,829	$287,790
Age 51	$8,000	$136,000	$40,736	$322,411
Age 52	$8,000	$144,000	$44,923	$360,148
Age 53	$8,000	$152,000	$49,416	$401,281
Age 54	$8,000	$160,000	$54,243	$446,116
Age 55	$8,000	$168,000	$59,432	$494,987
Age 56	$8,000	$176,000	$65,018	$548,256
Age 57	$8,000	$184,000	$71,035	$606,319
Age 58	$8,000	$192,000	$77,522	$669,607
Age 59	$8,000	$200,000	$84,522	$738,592
Age 60	$8,000	$208,000	$92,080	$813,785
Age 61	$8,000	$216,000	$100,248	$895,746
Age 62	$8,000	$224,000	$109,079	$985,083
Age 63	$8,000	$232,000	$118,635	$1,082,460
Age 64	$8,000	$240,000	$128,979	$1,188,602

Note: This illustration assumes consistent 9.0% Rate of Return with no down years in 401K earnings or mutual fund performance. This is the best case scenario one could could expect from continuously being invested in mutual funds. Values are shown on an end of year basis and assume contributions through age 64, retirement begins at age 65.

When the Johnson's begin to access these funds, however, they will be heavily taxed. Which begs the question: Will the Johnson's Qualified Retirement Plan Survive? (See the Chart, on page 19, for the answer.)

Will the Johnson's Qualified Retirement Plan Survive?

Let's fast forward to age 65 when the Johnson's will retire. The following chart shows what will happen to the Johnson's retirement fund when they begin to withdraw funds.

Currently, the Johnson's earn about $80,000 per year in combined income. Taking inflation into account, 30 years from now they will require $202,089 each year to maintain the same standard of living that they enjoy today. They will, however, be forced to withdraw a substantially larger amount ($252,111) to ensure they can pay the taxes they owe each year. They pay $50,522 that first year and receive a net amount of $202,089 to live on. The most shocking aspect of this chart is the fact that the Johnson's deplete all of their funds in slightly less than 6 years. Moreover, they paid out $288,800 in taxes whereas deductions on the contributions they made over that 30 year period were estimated to be $72,000. They paid back 4 times the amount of the benefit they received in the prior 30; only 6 years into retirement!

Name: Mr. and Mrs. Johnson

Current Age: 35 Ret. Age: 65 Years Money to Grow: 30

Present Value of QRP:	$8,000		
Annual Contributions:	$8,000	Rate of Inflation:	3.50%
Expected ROR	9.00%	Years:	30
Inflation Rate:	3.50%	Future Value Needed to Match:	$202,089
Current Annual Income:	$80,000	Present Value (Income after Contrib):	$ 72,000
Contribution Tax Deductions - Estimated:	$72,000	Heirs Marginal Tax Bracket:	30%
		Est. Retirement Marginal Tax Bracket:	20%

After Tax Net Annual Income: $202,089 Start Withdraw At Age: 65

Year	Age	IRA Balance	IRA Withdraw	Taxes Paid	Net After Tax Withdraw	IRA Balance After Withdraw	Net to Heirs After Tax
1	65	$ 1,188,602	$ 252,611	$ 50,522	$ 202,089	$ 935,991	$ 655,193
2	66	$ 1,020,230	$ 252,611	$ 50,522	$ 202,089	$ 767,618	$ 537,333
3	67	$ 836,704	$ 252,611	$ 50,522	$ 202,089	$ 584,092	$ 408,865
4	68	$ 636,661	$ 252,611	$ 50,522	$ 202,089	$ 384,049	$ 268,835
5	69	$ 418,614	$ 252,611	$ 50,522	$ 202,089	$ 166,002	$ 116,202
6	70	$ 180,943	$ 180,943	$ 36,189	$ 144,754	$ -	$ -
7	71	$ -	$ -	$ -	$ -	$ -	$ -
8	72	$ -	$ -	$ -	$ -	$ -	$ -
9	73	$ -	$ -	$ -	$ -	$ -	$ -
10	74	$ -	$ -	$ -	$ -	$ -	$ -
11	75	$ -	$ -	$ -	$ -	$ -	$ -
12	76	$ -	$ -	$ -	$ -	$ -	$ -
13	77	$ -	$ -	$ -	$ -	$ -	$ -
14	78	$ -	$ -	$ -	$ -	$ -	$ -
		TOTALS:	$1,444,000	$ 288,800	$1,155,200		

You may argue that they should just choose to live on a smaller amount of money each year. The authors would tell you that while this is an option, it is not advisable to plan for your future in that way. Changing the vehicle, in which you invest, instead of planning to cut back in the future, would be <u>our</u> recommendation.

In the past, most individuals considered these plans to be sound investments that would grow safely and relatively risk free. During the time period these plans were being developed, the financial institutions on Wall Street recognized billions of dollars were being made available for portfolio management. They seized the opportunity to create mutual funds that were made up of stock purchases. Each and every stock transaction earned the management company a commission regardless of the positive or negative performance of any client's investment.

Depositors were unaware of the volatility of the investment vehicle they were using for their retirement funds. "Black Monday" (Monday, October 19, 1987) and "911" (Tuesday, September 11, 2001) were historical dates when billions of dollars in retirement funds, "disappeared" over night. In actuality, money invested in the stock market is never really lost; it is simply transferred to another investor. Investing or trading the market is referred to as a 'zero sum game' because, technically, there are two sides to every trade. In every transaction, where there is an investor who sustains a loss, there is an investor on 'the other side of the trade' who makes a gain. The 'trick', if you will, is learning how to stay on the right side of the market in any investment. That is easier said than done, unless you make a continuous, intense study of the market.

Today, most employees jokingly refer to their 401(k) as their new 101(k) plan because it has decreased in value by an alarming amount. Educated investors know that investing in the stock market can be **risky**. But, why hasn't the typical employee taken this into consideration? They are choosing to contribute into a plan that runs the risk of **losing** a major portion of the principal invested. We believe that lack of information and lack of market education are the likely culprits leading employees down this risky path.

The chart below depicts the growth of $100,000. We have illustrated actual Stock Market returns using the S&P 500 Index from 1996 through 2005. For comparison, we have chosen a Steady Alternative illustrated at 12.0%. (Note: A 12.0% taxable rate of return is the equivalent of 9.0% after tax, assuming a 25% tax bracket.)

Of course, stock market returns come with the risk of loss of principal. Over time, an investment that protects your principal will serve you well. Note the $59,476 difference the Steady Alternative provides (see below).

Stock Market Returns versus Steady Alternative

Year	S&P 500	$100,000 Investment	Steady Alternative	$100,000 Investment
1996	35.2%	$135,200	12%	$112,000
1997	23.6%	$167,121	12%	$125,440
1998	24.7%	$208,383	12%	$140,493
1999	30.5%	$272,023	12%	$157,352
2000	8.9%	$296,097	12%	$176,234
2001	-1.9%	$290,382	12%	$197,382
2002	-17.3%	$240,262	12%	$221,068
2003	-24.3%	$181,903	12%	$247,596
2004	32.2%	$240,457	12%	$277,308
2005	4.4%	**$251,109**	12%	**$310,585**
	Difference:	**$59,476**		

Some individuals are able to establish qualified Roth IRA's. Although these types of retirement accounts allow for larger contributions, they still come with certain limitations.

There is a better way!

For many years, wealthy individuals have practiced the concepts being taught in this book. They put this knowledge to work for them and structured a plan, similar to the plan you will put into place for yourself. The type of investment vehicle we recommend is much safer. It minimizes risk of principal loss and in most cases provides a higher, tax exempt rate of return. (Remember, you always want to pay taxes on the seed, not the harvest!)

INTEREST EXPENSES

Your enemy or best friend!

Interest expense is a topic many people misunderstand when it comes to financial planning. Earlier, we stated we would discuss the differences between good debt and bad debt and how one serves to destroy wealth, while the other assists in wealth creation.

The amount of credit card debt in our country is at an all time high. We are bombarded with television, radio and direct mail advertising from companies that will provide you with all the money you need because of your good credit history. Buy now, pay later promotions convince us we can have it all today and put off paying until tomorrow. We are literally being brain washed with the idea of accumulating debt to support a great life style.

What is happening is catastrophic to our financial well being. People are being fooled into spending their future income and savings. Worse yet, they are not planning for the inevitable. Eventually, all this debt will need to be paid. This is an example of bad debt that can serve to derail your plan of wealth creation. In most cases, the interest charges on these accounts are at extremely high rates and the interest is not tax deductible.

If you discuss interest charges with any business owner, he/she will tell you interest charges are a necessary part of financing their business operations. However, in this instance, the interest charges are tax deductible expenses and can be used to offset profits of the company. This is an example of good debt. The business loan helps the business to grow and the interest expense is used to the advantage of the business in calculating taxes owed at the end of the year.

Another example of good debt is a person's home mortgage. All mortgage payments include an interest rate charged for the duration of the mortgage. The interest paid is an expense that can work in favor of the buyer because it helps to reduce the amount of income taxes that will be owed at the end of each year. Many people purchase a home with the idea in mind that it is a good long-term investment. In terms of wealth creation and retirement planning, the interest expense can be a significant factor. Later we will demonstrate how to use the interest expense on a mortgage to help accelerate the growth of your investment portfolio.

A sound financial plan should always include a plan for eliminating all bad, debt. Any type of interest expense that depletes money, you would otherwise save, only serves to stall your wealth creation efforts.

Automobile purchases are a necessary part of one's normal expenditures. We can show you how to implement a strategy to purchase that vehicle and actually make a nice profit just by structuring the purchase differently. As you progress through your plan, you will learn how to use this type of purchase to your advantage.

YOUR SECRET WEAPON FOR CREATING WEALTH

Throughout the years, there has been a lot of information published about how a home purchase can be a major factor in overall financial planning. Home ownership has been a significant part of The American Dream for many decades. For many families, it will be the single, largest asset that is ever purchased.

Your secret weapon for creating wealth is your **home equity**. The proper management of home equity can be extremely powerful. You should treat the management of your home equity as though it were a profitable business. The concepts introduced, here, can greatly accelerate the growth of your financial portfolio. Our goal is to show you how to make home equity work for you; instead of you working for your home equity.

Our grandparents taught our parents, by the time of retirement, they should have their home mortgages paid in full. Many of them paid off their mortgages much sooner. By tradition, our parents taught us to do exactly the same. The days of the "Great Depression" served as a grim reminder of when so many, hard working families lost their homes to banks due to unexpected unemployment. Those affected certainly did not want a repeat of that event in their lifetimes or their children's lives. On page 10, we indicated why paying off the mortgage as soon as possible was "rock solid advice" for them.

Now for the challenge! Open your mind to completely change your idea about properly managing HOME EQUITY. How much more effectively could you increase your wealth and grow retirement funds if you were able to use your home equity as an effective financial growth tool?

What is the rate of return you earn on your home equity? Let's say you purchased a home and invested twenty percent of the purchase price as a down payment. (Remember our parents and grandparents taught us to finance it this way.) The purchase price of the home was $200,000, so, your down payment was $40,000. Assume that your home has appreciated by 20% since your original purchase and you have borrowed no additional money against the home equity. You, now, have a total of $80,000 in equity. How much is that $80,000 earning on a yearly basis? The answer to that question is ZERO, ZILCH, NADA!

Many people mistakenly believe, by reducing the amount of principal owed on their home, they are increasing their equity and therefore putting themselves into a better financial situation. For that same reason, there are even some individual homeowners who make extra payments each year just for the sole purpose of reducing the principal amount owed. What they don't understand is this is not a prudent manner in which to manage their extra money. Regardless of the extra payments made, the monthly mortgage payments remain the same until the mortgage is finally paid in full. Think about this for a moment! What the homeowner has succeeded in doing is very good for the bank, but not good for the homeowner! Every time an extra payment is made to reduce the principal amount of the mortgage, the homeowner is actually lending, free money to the bank. The bank never asked for the extra payment and they have no obligation to pay interest on the extra funds. Although the homeowner might not get a very high rate of return, he/she would be better off by placing the amount of the extra payments into a regular savings account. At least, then, they would be earning some interest on those extra funds.

Properly managing your home equity is no different than managing any other sound investment. Regardless of investment type, savvy investors concern themselves with protecting the principal amount invested. They attempt to get the highest rate of return possible and they are always concerned about the liquidity of the investment. In other words, how quickly can they get their money from the investment in the event of a financial emergency? Your management of home equity should take the same investment parameters into consideration.

We teach you it is far better to grow your financial portfolio in a manner that will provide you with the ability to pay off your home mortgage in full, IF YOU CHOOSE to do so. Soon, you will understand why it is far better to always have your home, 100% mortgaged - if at all possible.

Let's look at an example of not investing wisely! Joe and Mary are excited to start a new business that requires them to purchase a new delivery vehicle. They purchase the vehicle with cash and the very next day they take it to work and park it. Instead, they use one of their personal vehicles to make the deliveries. Day after day, the newly purchased delivery vehicle sits completely idle. They paid cash for the vehicle, but it is not helping them in their business and, therefore, not providing any rate of return on investment. Although this seems like a ridiculous example, it is exactly what most people do when it comes to home equity. In essence, they have their home equity parked and sitting idle! At Wealth2020, Inc. we meet people on a daily basis, who have $50,000, $100,000 and sometimes as much as $500,000 or more in home equity that is earning nothing. This idle equity is no different from the new vehicle that was purchased and parked. It is a bad investment!

Wouldn't it be a better idea, to convert that equity to cash, and then place the cash into an investment vehicle that earns a greater rate of return than the increased amount of mortgage payments? You bet it would! Because, then, the equity is working for you instead of sitting idle. In financial terms, this is referred to as arbitrage. It is the method banks have used to make fortunes for centuries. In a later chapter, titled "Arbitrage" we will go into more detail and explain how to apply this concept to create more wealth in your portfolio.

For now, let's look at the following flowchart. It depicts one of the advantages of separating equity from your home. As you can see, the net effect of taking out the equity is an annual increase in one's savings of $5,100, taking into account, the interest tax deduction associated with the loan. By simply repositioning an idle asset, you effectively increase your annual savings. This is what we call free money as you would not pay anything, out of pocket, to accomplish this. What would an additional $5,100 in annual savings do for your family? (See the exponential growth of this amount, over time, on the next page.)

Using Equity To Create Wealth

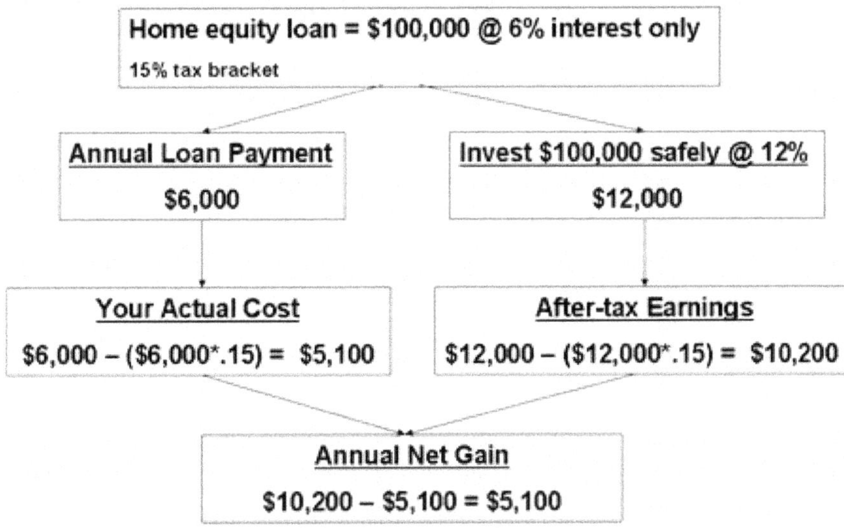

The following chart shows the compounding effect of the $5,100 per year gain in savings. On a year by year basis, you are earning $5,100 and you are also earning a return on your earnings from prior years - this is the magic of compounding!

After 15 Years Of FREE Money Growth

Year	Rate	Annual Growth
1	12%	$5,100
2	12%	$10,812
3	12%	$17,209
4	12%	$24,375
5	**12%**	**$32,400**
6	12%	$41,387
10	**12%**	**$89,499**
11	12%	$105,338
15	**12%**	**$190,127**

$100,000
+ $190,127
290,127

Your Benefit
Ability to pay off house EARLY

This example assumes that we start with a $300,000 home. The original outstanding loan on the home is $190,000. We borrowed $100,000 of equity and invested it at 12%. As you can see, by year 15, you have the ability to pay off the home in full. (The original $100,000 you took from home equity, plus the $190,127 you earned on the equity you took out, makes this entirely possible.) We will always maintain it is better to have the ability to pay off your home at any time rather than actually paying it off. Separate the equity from your home to maintain safety, liquidity of your funds and to earn a rate of return on an idle asset; and, lastly to maintain one of your best tax deductions – the mortgage interest deduction. By making one small change in your finances, you position yourself for financial freedom.

The most exciting aspect of the previous chart is the fact it is quite conservative. If you were to harvest an additional $20,000 to $30,000 from your home equity every 5 years or so, you could expect to explode your savings. When you separate the equity from your home, you increase your ability to pay off the mortgage more quickly than if you kept equity in the home. There are numerous other benefits to separating your equity as discussed above.

AN IMPORTANT NOTE! There are many homeowners who refinance their home with the sole purpose of using the money to purchase depreciating assets such as a boat, vacation or automobile. This is another example of bad debt. You do not want to fall into this serious financial trap. Later in the book, the chapter titled "Becoming Your Own Banker" demonstrates a method that provides the funds to make the same purchases, but in a way more profitable to you. The method we reveal will assist you in growing your net worth instead of depleting your net worth.

Safety and protection of principal is a strong component of any good investment. If managing your home equity is similar to managing any other good investment, then you should be aware of the safety ramifications of accumulating large amounts of home equity that is sitting idle. Your equity is at risk!

Home foreclosures are at an all time high in many geographic areas of the United States. Although there are many homeowners who have completely mismanaged their finances and caused their own financial problems, there are also many homeowners, who, through no fault of their own, have lost their homes in foreclosure. They might have experienced an unforeseen catastrophic illness, a death of one of the wage earners in the family or an extended period of unexpected unemployment. So what if this should suddenly happen to you? How safe is your equity if you were faced with a foreclosure because you could not make your monthly mortgage payments on time?

Unfortunately, many homeowners are conditioned to believe it is best to accumulate equity as quickly as possible in their haste to pay off their homes. Once they are faced with an unforeseen financial hardship, they go to their bank to get a loan and quickly learn, because of late payments and the guidelines of the bank, they are unable to borrow against the property. Even if the homeowner has a track record of making extra principal payments during good financial times; this argument is not sufficient to convince the bank to lend the homeowner the money. The homeowner goes into foreclosure and loses all their equity. NOT VERY SAFE, IS IT? We teach people to separate their home equity for the purpose of creating wealth (as demonstrated on page 25.) We also want you to conserve the equity in the form of solid and safe investments that have liquidity in the event of an unexpected financial crisis.

What if you were that person facing a financial crisis? Prior to that event, you purchased this book and decided to apply the principles outlined to grow your financial portfolio. You refinanced your home, took out a large portion, if not all, of the equity and kept it protected in a safe and liquid investment. Suddenly, you are faced with an unforeseen financial crisis. But, instead of panicking, you now have money available to keep your mortgage payments current. Guess what! You, instead of the bank, are now in control of the equity because you converted it to cash and manage it in a safe investment that is liquid.

A common situation, families face during their prime income earning years, is relocation, due to a job change. Many times the families have accumulated a considerable amount of equity in their home. In order to get the cash from the property, they must wait until the house sells. If the market conditions are such, that home sales in the area are exceptionally slow, the sellers are faced with the realism of selling it at a reduced price, in order to sell it quickly.

If, instead, they had refinanced the house and separated out their equity prior to their move, they would have increased their options for selling the property. These options would include selling via a lease/option contract, renting the property or possibly selling via a subject-to-existing financing contract. Most homeowners make the mistake of assuming if the home does not sell right away, they will be able to refinance *after* an attempt to sell the home. This is a bad assumption! Almost all mortgage companies will check to see if the house has been listed for sale within the last six months. If it has been listed during that time, they will not refinance the property. Mortgage companies, learned by experience that many homeowners faced with hard times and stressful situations are not adverse to abandoning properties, once they realize they are not able to receive the necessary sales price for their home. This is especially true if the homeowner has **no equity** left in the property.

Unlike our grandparents, statistics show the average American family will live in the same home for only 7.2 years. We find people move for many reasons; sometimes it is a job transfer. It could be the family is growing larger because they are having more children or maybe they simply wish to move to another part of town. Whatever the reason, the change of lifestyle should be taken into consideration when you are structuring your long-term financial plan. Here is the reason why!

A traditional thirty year mortgage with a 7.5% interest rate will cause the homeowner to pay almost 2.5 times the original amount borrowed. That means a $100,000 mortgage will eventually cost the homeowner approximately $252,000 in thirty years if they live in the home the entire time. So how much is paid on the principal after 15 years? It is astounding to see that, after 15 years, only 25% of the principal amount has been paid. In 7.2 years (the average time spent in a home), the percentage paid to principal is much less. An important note! Profit earned from purchasing a home is not derived by reducing principal. Profit is earned, when market conditions cause the house to appreciate and it is sold for more money than the original purchase price.

During the educational Financial Wellness System™, seminars we conduct, we explain to attendees the subject of our seminars is not intended to be about mortgages. However, we do stress when you make a home purchase, you should pay close attention to the type of mortgage you use. The terms and interest rate of the mortgage will affect the results of your long-term financial goals.

Consider the financial implications of the following scenario. You set out to increase your net worth by purchasing a home that accumulates equity with improving real estate market conditions. You understand very little of your monthly payment will be applied toward reducing principal and you expect to move within the average time of 7.2 years. Ask yourself why you would be concerned about making principal payments? After all, by applying the information in this book, you fully comprehend you always want the ability to pay off your mortgage, in full, if you so choose.

After you finish reading this book, you will realize how important it is to consider the advantages of purchasing your home with an interest only loan as compared to using a traditional, fully amortized, 30 year loan. Note! The market place continually changes and new mortgage products are introduced daily. Make sure you find a good mortgage company that will review all the products to find the best one for your situation.

Interest charges are a necessary part of your mortgage. You should accept these charges and, most of all, should consider these charges as your friend and not your enemy! In the previous chapter, "The Ticking Tax Bomb", we noted one factor which will affect the amount of taxes you will pay during retirement is the loss of an interest deduction for a home mortgage. Interest paid on your mortgage is a tax-deductible expense. The deduction can be used to offset the taxes you will pay as your income increases and you are pushed into a higher income tax bracket. The information in the following chapters will go into more detail about how the correct loan will help you build a solid financial plan using equity and putting it to work for you. The most important point to remember is interest expense, used properly in your financial wealth building plan, can actually be your friend.

This chapter focused on the power of using home equity to create wealth. Successful real estate investors understand this concept and use it to consistently put together very profitable real estate transactions. As you begin to implement your new financial growth strategies, you should strive to master more of the details involved with this important concept.

The topic of properly managing your home equity is covered thoroughly in the book, "Missed Fortune 101," authored by Douglas R. Andrew. We highly recommend you purchase and read the book so you gain an understanding of the finer points of this concept.

THE POWER OF ARBITRAGE

Arbitrage! The word itself has such a mystical connotation. Applying the principles of arbitrage as a strategic tool to create wealth is actually not mystical at all. Banks have used arbitrage for centuries. As a matter of fact, banks would not exist without it! The principles of arbitrage are pure common sense and very straight forward. *How can it work for you?*

Here is how it works! Mega Bucks Bank advertises for depositors to invest money into their savings account program. The bank pays the depositor a small amount of interest. The bank then lends that money to other credit-worthy customers. However, the amount of interest charged to the borrower is considerably higher. The difference between the amount paid to the depositor and the amount collected from the borrower is arbitrage or the gross profit earned by the bank. In some cases, the difference in percentages between the two transactions might seem to be quite small, but when you take into consideration these transactions are made up of thousands of depositors and borrowers, each year, the amount earned is absolutely staggering. That is why you see new banks being built on almost every street corner!

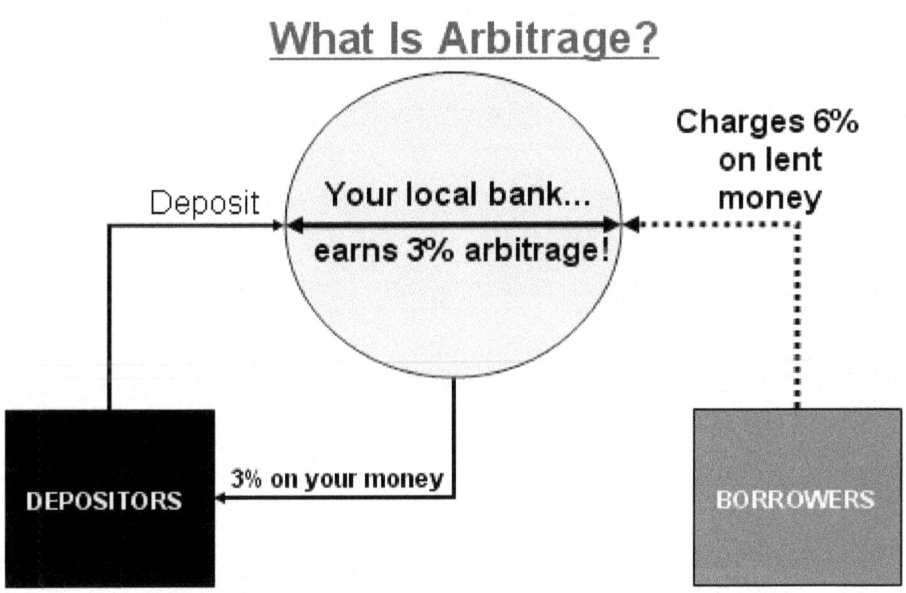

Now for the exciting part! As you master the principles of using arbitrage, you will accelerate the growth of your personal wealth building system. The importance of using arbitrage cannot be overstated. Throughout the years, it will be one of the most powerful financial tools in your wealth building arsenal. Despite what appear to be very small percentage differences between money borrowed and money earned, the effects of compounding these small amounts over time have an exponential impact on any investment. Remember, "You must learn to crawl before you walk and you must learn to walk before you run". For this reason, we want you to begin thinking of the possibilities of applying arbitrage with small percentage differences of 2-5 percent. Later, as we discuss high yield investment opportunities you will learn how to run, so-to-speak, with percentages that are much larger.

Before we continue, it might be appropriate to review the basic topics covered in our book, to this point. So far we covered how important it is for you to define your goals. Be certain to write out your goals, so you can review them on a daily basis. As you get into the habit of reviewing them, you will see how much easier it is to follow your new plan that will lead you to financial prosperity.

We discussed the Great American Dream and how the financial rules changed. You now have a better understanding of why you must endeavor to create wealth within your prime income earning years. The chapter describing the unfortunate facts of life shows us the importance of creating a financial plan that incorporates life insurance protection to assure the financial well being of your loved ones, in the event of your premature death. The subsequent chapters covered the ticking tax bomb associated with the taxes you will pay as you withdraw funds from your current IRA and 401(k) plans. Next, we covered the advantages and disadvantages of interest expenses and finally, we discussed the power of managing your home equity and mastering the concept of arbitrage. Now it is time to bring all these concepts together to formulate your future plan!

THE MOST OVERLOOKED INVESTMENT TOOL

In 2000, I (Jerry) formed a partnership with a custom home builder. The local real estate market was strong, so we decided to build a custom home and sell it for profit.

Proper planning is absolutely critical to the success of building a custom home. All the elements of a building plan might seem overwhelming, but when you sit down and outline them in the order necessary to proceed, it's really not that difficult. You determine a budget for costs, pick out an architectural design, purchase a parcel of land that fits the design, hire a good builder, arrange construction financing and set a date to begin.

In order to proceed with the construction of a new home, all the plans and drawings must conform to local building standards within the governing, county agencies. The very first plan that is reviewed is the foundation for the home. The foundation must be professionally designed and engineered to coincide with the soil conditions present at the building site. This one element is so important, no other plans or drawings are approved until the foundation plans and drawings have been properly reviewed and approved.

Your future wealth building plan will require you to think in terms, just as if you were building a house. You will build upon a solid foundation so there is never any guess work as to whether your plan will achieve the results you intended.

As you completed the last chapter, dealing with arbitrage, you were presented with a summary of all the subjects of the previous chapters. Up until this point they have been described as separate and distinct elements of your future wealth building system. Together they will become the essential building blocks for your plan. Now we are ready to show you how to build the foundation for your long-term financial plan!

Life Insurance! It is commonly one of the most misunderstood financial tools used for creating wealth. However, it is one of the most powerful financial tools available to you. Earlier we stated an integral part of your planning would include the use of a properly structured INVESTMENT GRADE LIFE INSURANCE contract. At the beginning of this book, we asked you to keep an open mind to new concepts. Utilizing the **correct type** of life insurance will require a thorough understanding of this concept.

Purchasing a life insurance contract is, by far, one of the most overlooked methods used to accelerate growth in a family's financial plan. Once you master the concepts taught in this chapter, you will understand why wealthy families have used this, little advertised tool, for more than one hundred years. Like many of our clients, you will probably be asking the question, "Why haven't other financial planners ever introduced me to this highly effective wealth building strategy?" It is as though these concepts are part of some deep dark secret! At this juncture of our book, let us emphasize, it is not important why the concepts have not been introduced to you in the past. What is important is the concepts work equally, if not more, effectively today than they ever did in the past! Let me re-emphasize the last statement. Using a life insurance contract as the foundation of your wealth building system, works more effectively than almost any other system you can employ!

So, what is the life insurance product that holds the keys to your financial success? It is a unique product called an Equity Indexed Universal Life Contract! There are literally hundreds of different types of life insurance plans to consider. What separates this type of plan from all others is that it is classified as an INVESTMENT GRADE product! Most other life insurance products are structured with one purpose in mind and one purpose only! They are designed to provide a cash benefit to your heirs in the event of your un-timely death. With traditional products, you are advised to purchase the most death benefit for the least possible amount of premium invested. A more appropriate name for this type of coverage might be death insurance.

The Equity Indexed Universal Life, (EIUL) contract works exactly the opposite. It provides a living benefit that goes on into perpetuity, which simply means until the time of your death. As people are generally living longer, this is an excellent benefit for policy holders. The product assists with the management and growth of your retirement funds in addition to allowing you to manage and participate in other high yield investment opportunities. In order to optimize cash accumulation values, within the EIUL contract, a computer program is used to solve for the smallest amount of death benefit with the largest amount of premium.

Typical reactions upon introducing this concept, to new clients, are: "I don't think I need more life insurance. Or, I didn't know life insurance could be used to create wealth!" These reactions are perfectly understandable. We explain to our clients that the EIUL contract is one of the **most effective** wealth creation vehicles. The death benefit coverage is a significant side benefit that comes with the contract.

At Wealth2020, Inc., we work with clients from one end of the financial spectrum to the other. Basically the clients fall into three categories. Some are beginning a career right out of college or high school and are looking for financial guidance for the next 30 to 40 years. Others have already attained financial success and are looking for a method to disperse excess funds to heirs on a tax-free basis. Most clients are mid-stream in their life and are not satisfied with the growth of their financial portfolio. They are looking for a viable investment alternative that works. Although the stages of development in their financial plan are different, the strategies outlined in this book work equally well for all three categories of clients.

Developing your plan! Like building a house, you must first define your long-term financial goals. Once you establish your goals you will implement a plan to reach them. Please, don't under estimate this first step. It has been stated many times that people don't plan to fail they fail to plan. Henry Ford once said, "If you think you can do a thing or you think you can't do a thing, you're right."

You are actually going to begin building your plan by working 'backwards.' In that manner, you will determine approximately how much money you will need to live comfortably during your retirement years. You will factor in both the rate of inflation and the income tax rate that will affect your net proceeds.

Remember the chapter that spoke about the ticking tax bomb? By using a traditional 401(k) or IRA, everyone is prolonging the inevitable, so they will eventually pay taxes on the harvest instead of the seed. As a better alternative, you are going to learn how to save for retirement by using an EIUL contract that will allow you to fund the policy with after tax dollars and later withdraw the income proceeds, completely tax-free. Your tax consequences will be much less, or better yet, non existent! This one element of the contract makes a huge difference in your net, spendable income. Remember, if you are in a 30% tax bracket at the time of retirement a $50,000 per year, tax-free income is the equivalent of a pre-tax income of approximately $71,500.

The correct life insurance contract is one of the very few investment vehicles that can legally provide this type of tax-free benefit, as per IRS guidelines. But, it gets even better! The contract allows you to manage your funds without the many restrictions imposed via traditional IRA's or 401(k)'s. The major benefits associated with funding the EIUL contract are as follows.

- Never lose principal
- Financial protection in the event of your premature death
- More income at time of retirement
- Tax-free retirement income
- Contribution amounts not restricted
- Loans from the policy do not restrict the use of funds
- Management of funds within the policy provide the opportunity for creating Arbitrage

From this day forward, you should view your retirement in a totally different light. You are going to manage your retirement as though it were a highly profitable business. You will be in control of the funds, not a money manager who makes money regardless of the proper or improper management of your funds.

The subject of wealth creation vehicles and retirement savings plans is often times controversial. We are all constantly inundated with advertising that promotes stocks, mutual funds and other financial products. These are usually sold by banks or brokerage firms. Although, there is a sense of security that is promoted with these products, there is probably no safer investment vehicle than that of a life insurance contract; especially if you are purchasing the contract from a top rated insurance company.

Insurance companies are, without question, the most stable financial institutions in the world. In fact, they are the backbone of the economy. It is a little known fact, insurance companies bailed out many of the failing banks during the time of the Great Depression. They are regulated by a much higher set of standards than those of financial institutions such as banks. Insurance companies are required to keep $1.05 in reserves, for every dollar on deposit; while banks are only required to have approximately $0.15 in reserves, for every dollar on deposit.

Certain life insurance contracts are considered to be investment grade vehicles because they receive tax-favored status. Under certain sections of the IRS Code, the accumulation, of cash value, inside an insurance contract is tax-advantaged. That means, unlike investments in mutual funds and stocks, your money is able to grow within the insurance contract completely tax-free. Structured properly, you will be able to access the funds at a later date, all without paying taxes. Your withdrawals will be structured in the form of annual loans, from the policy, at the time of retirement. This is why it is such a powerful investment tool!

So what about rates of return? During the bull market of the mid to late 90's many investors bragged about the phenomenal returns they were earning on their stock portfolio. Very few investors anticipated the collapse of the market in 2000. Not only did many investors lose the gain on their previous investments, but they also lost a major portion of their principal. It is interesting to note, when an investor suffers a 40% loss in their portfolio, it requires more than a 40% gain on the remaining dollars to make up the loss. It requires almost 67% returns on the remaining dollars in order to get back to a break-even point. It is sad to hear of individuals who invested their life savings, then suffered a major loss and were forced back to where they originally started many years before.

One of the primary advantages of investing via an investment grade life insurance contract is your principal is guaranteed. Insurance companies recognize that investors are looking for safety and have developed these products in response to that need. In order to be competitive, they offer products that project safe rates of return of approximately 7%-9%. These returns actually equate to 10%-13% pre-tax, for a person who is in or approaching a 30% tax bracket. When you take this tax-favored status into consideration, the products become highly competitive. Since the principal is guaranteed against loss and funds accumulate tax-free; it becomes an **un-beatable** investment vehicle!

Now that you are familiar with the tax advantages of an EIUL contract, let's take a look at how to properly fund your policy. The only restriction on the amount of money you are allowed to invest is dictated by your personal budget. However, there are provisions of the IRS code that establish guidelines as to how quickly you are able to fund the policy. In 1982, the Tax and Fiscal Responsibility Act (TEFRA) was passed and in 1984, the Deficit Reduction Act (DEFRA) was passed. Both acts were passed to establish the parameters that dictate the minimum amount of death benefit required for a cash-value life insurance policy that is being used for tax-free capital accumulation.

The Technical and Miscellaneous Revenue Act (TAMRA), which was passed by congress and put into law (June 21, 1988) also establishes the guidelines with regard to how quickly you can fund an EIUL contract. As long as all these parameters are met, the EIUL contract will provide the tax-advantaged status that allows you tax-free access to your funds. That's where Wealth2020, Inc. comes in. We ensure your policy is structured and maintained according to these regulations at all times.

Once our clients understand how effectively this process works, many of them decide to reposition large amounts of assets. You might decide to do the same for the following reason. Did you realize that a lump sum of money grows faster than investing the exact same amount over a period of time? Refer to the chart, **Lump-Sum versus Periodic Payments,** on page 35. This chart illustrates the results achieved when investing a lump sum of $100,000 versus investing the same amount of money in equal monthly payments over an extended period of time. You can see, within ten years, there is a dramatic difference of $81,832.

Lump-Sum versus Periodic Payments

	10 Years	15 Years	20 Years	25 Years
$100k lump sum invested (9% compounded annually)	**$245,136**	**$383,804**	**$600,915**	**$940,841**
$833.33/month invested ($100K total invested) (9% compounded annually)	**$163,304**	**$255,682**	**$400,316**	**$626,768**
Difference is Lump-Sum Advantage:	**$81,832**	**$128,122**	**$200,599**	**$314,073**

We've explained how important it is to maximize your wealth creation plan by properly managing home equity. Many of our clients have accumulated substantial amounts of home equity because they thought it was a wise investment strategy. They understand the power of investing a larger lump sum, so they separate the equity from their home and use it to fund an EIUL contract.

Let's assume you are able to access $250,000 by refinancing your home. You would then be able to fund the EIUL contract in increments of $50,000, each year, for five years. *Why does it take 5 years?* In order to conform to TAMRA guidelines, the EIUL contract must be funded in equal yearly increments for not less than five years. If a contract is not funded properly, with care taken to maintain its tax advantaged status, it creates a tax consequence with the policy known as a Modified Endowment Contract (MEC). A MEC policy does not have the same tax advantages as that of a properly structured EIUL contract. Please don't let any of these legal terms scare you. Our only purpose for introducing them is so you are aware these guidelines exist.

An educated investor will quickly realize that the increase in monthly mortgage payments could offset potential gains. However, keep in mind that repositioning equity is only one of the building blocks of your foundation. Increased interest expense will become an advantage to you, in terms of tax deductions, and will serve to minimize the difference in the increase of monthly payments.

Wealth2020, Inc. works with clients in different stages of their investment careers. Due to financial limitations, many younger families find they must fund their EIUL contract over an extended period of time. That is great! Understand that incremental amounts also grow to fantastic sums over time. Regardless of your current financial situation, just get started. **Procrastination is your worst enemy!**

Throughout our book, we advise you to view the development of your long-term plan as though you are managing a profitable business. Let's stop for a minute and discuss the topic of **Cash Flow versus Profit**. Occasionally, individuals lose sight of their goals when they see money going out, with none coming in. Don't let this happen to you! Successful business owners know that investing money in their business is often times one of the most lucrative methods they can use to earn high rates of return on their dollars invested. Investing cash (out-going **cash flow**), to support the business is done for the purpose of increasing the long-term revenues (**profit**) of the business. The money invested is often derived from long-term business loans. In similar terms, you are removing equity from your home, converting it to cash, investing it into your wealth creation business in order to generate long-term high rates of return. Your monthly payments (out-going **cash flow**) supports the generation of future tax-free retirement income (**profit**). This one business principle reinforces why using equity is such a powerful tool for creating wealth.

You may recognize when you re-finance and separate equity to fund the EIUL contract, there will be funds that have not yet been re-positioned. Due to the 5-year provisions of TAMRA, for funding the contract, only one fifth of the funds will be used in the first year. Therefore, at the beginning of year one, $200,000 will be unused. In year two, $150,000 remains unused. The unused funds, decrease in increments of $50,000 until the beginning of year, five. In a later chapter dealing with high yield investments, we will demonstrate how to position the remaining funds to provide higher returns while you are waiting to move them into the plan. By doing so, you will use arbitrage to further enhance the growth of your financial plan.

Home equity is only one asset that can be re-positioned. We work with clients who have large amounts of cash accumulated in IRA's or other retirement accounts that are performing poorly. Due to lack of principal protection, their funds decline in value over time. Once they understand the power of the EIUL plan, they elect to reposition the funds from those accounts in order to fund their revised financial plan with a larger infusion of cash, starting from day one.

Note! For those who are concerned about penalties, it is sometimes possible to roll out these assets and avoid the 10% penalty, even if you are pre age 59½. In nearly every case, it makes better investment sense to roll out the funds, pay the taxes and start growing your retirement funds in a tax-free, compounding environment. This is yet another example of paying taxes on the seed in order to avoid paying substantially more taxes on the harvest in later years. Please understand that you <u>will</u> pay taxes on these funds at some point in time anyhow. Make the smart choice to pay the least amount of taxes; by paying them now and enjoy your harvest tax-free.

Following, is an example of an individual who saw the extreme advantages to our wealth creating system. He elected to roll out his IRA, pay the taxes and the penalty; thus allowing him to superfund his policy. For this example, we estimated a 9% rate of return in his IRA. In the chart below, you can see that this individual had to pay taxes on the money rolled out at his marginal tax-rate of 32.5% and a 10% penalty as he is age 48. He chose to pay taxes and penalty now to gain a better position for retirement success.

IRA Balance at Rollout:	$ 127,500
Marginal Tax Rate:	32.50%
Years to Rollout:	5
Estimated Current Return:	9.0%
Current Age:	48
Age to Begin Rollout:	48

Future Value of IRA Calculator:

Estimated Return	9.0%
Number of Growth Years	0
Present Value	$ 127,500
Annual Payments:	$ -
Future Value:	$ 127,500

Year	Age	IRA Balance	IRA Rollout	Estimated Taxes Paid	New IRA Balance	Amount To Rollout
1	48	$ 127,500	$ 25,500	$ (10,838)	$ 102,000	$ 14,663
2	49	$ 111,180	$ 27,795	$ (11,813)	$ 83,385	$ 15,982
3	50	$ 90,890	$ 30,297	$ (12,876)	$ 60,593	$ 17,421
4	51	$ 66,046	$ 33,023	$ (14,035)	$ 33,023	$ 18,988
5	52	$ 35,995	$ 35,995	$ (15,298)	$ -	$ 20,697
6	53	$ -	$ -	$ -	$ -	$ -
7	54	$ -	$ -	$ -	$ -	$ -
8	55	$ -	$ -	$ -	$ -	$ -
9	56	$ -	$ -	$ -	$ -	$ -
10	57	$ -	$ -	$ -	$ -	$ -
11	58	$ -	$ -	$ -	$ -	$ -
12	59	$ -	$ -	$ -	$ -	$ -
13	60	$ -	$ -	$ -	$ -	$ -
14	61	$ -	$ -	$ -	$ -	$ -
15	62	$ -	$ -	$ -	$ -	$ -
16	63	$ -	$ -	$ -	$ -	$ -
17	64	$ -	$ -	$ -	$ -	$ -
18	65	$ -	$ -	$ -	$ -	$ -
19	66	$ -	$ -	$ -	$ -	$ -
20	67	$ -	$ -	$ -	$ -	$ -
		TOTALS:	$ 152,610	$ (64,859)		$ 87,751

Let us note, this client left his previous employment and was now working for another company. He was unsatisfied with the growth of his funds which were being managed by the plan administrator of his former employer. He was more than willing to consider paying a penalty, once he saw the benefits associated with repositioning his assets.

We assisted him with calculating the future value of his funds and determined, with an aggressive rate of 9%, his funds would grow to approximately $549,609 at age 65 (if he left the funds in his current IRA.) Next, we demonstrated the tax consequences associated with leaving his funds in the qualified plan until retirement. Beginning at age 65 he would need to withdraw $81,685, before taxes in order to net the same amount of $65,348 per year which he would get from our plan. The biggest difference between staying with his current plan and switching to our plan is that with his plan he would run out of money in 9.5 years, whereas with our plan he would net $65,348 tax-free per year into perpetuity. In addition, he had the side benefit of insurance coverage in the amount of $686,036 in the event of premature death during and after his working years. This scenario demonstrates this individual's fate if he were to leave his funds in his IRA versus repositioning them into an EIUL. He gladly paid the taxes and penalty when he saw that he would likely run out of retirement funds by age 74. *Who wouldn't!?*

The **key** to making <u>all of this work</u> is repositioning assets. After our clients realize the power associated with this type of plan, they begin looking at how they might be able to double or triple their retirement income without investing much more money than they are already investing. Everyone's situation is different, but in almost all cases, this type of plan will always produce superior results for retirement without compromising the person's current lifestyle.

Note! When considering the roll-out of funds from an existing IRA or 401(k), there are many factors to consider. However, don't let yourself get hung up with early withdrawal penalties if you can see the end results will be more favorable by making that change. Sometimes a person needs to spend a dime in order to make a dollar! If you let time work in your favor, you will eventually end up being the winner.

Let's take a look at the illustration on page 39. This is part of the plan for the client we just referenced. Our client chose to reposition his IRA and $112,249 of home equity which was earning nothing for him. The plan was Superfunded over 5 years. A total of $200,000 repositioned, will provide him with a tax-free income of $65,348 beginning at age 66 and lasting into perpetuity. That is $81,685 per year on a pre-tax basis, assuming a 20% tax-bracket in retirement. The following illustration shows the results of restructuring his financial plan.

Designed for: Most Overlooked Tool	$686,036 Selected Face Amount
Issue Age: 48	Initial Annual Premium: $40,000.00
Male, Standard Non-Tobacco	Initial Death Benefit Option: Level

Supplemental Report Description: This report shows both the account value and cash surrender value, and lists the schedule of surrender charges for the illustrated policy.

							Non-Guaranteed Assumed			
End of Year	Age	Modal Premium	Times Per Year	Annual Premium	Cash From Policy	Annual Outlay	Surr Cash Value	Surr Charge	Account Value	Death Benefit
1	49	40,000	1	40,000	0	40,000	13.107	23.613	36,720	686,036
2	50	40,000	1	40,000	0	40,000	54.473	22.039	76,512	686,036
3	51	40,000	1	40,000	0	40,000	99.231	20.465	119,696	686,036
4	52	40,000	1	40.000	0	40,000	147.738	18.891	166,629	686,036
5	53	40,000	1	40,000	0	40,000	200.376	17.316	217,692	686,036
6	54	0	1	0	0	0	216.294	15.742	232,036	686,036
7	55	0	1	0	0	0	233.408	14.168	247,576	686,036
8	56	0	1	0	0	0	251.833	12.594	264,427	686,036
9	57	0	1	0	0	0	271.675	11.020	282,694	686,036
10	58	0	1	0	0	0	295.988	9.445	305,434	686,036
				200,000	0	200,000				
11	59	0	1	0	0	0	324.373	7.871	332,245	686,036
12	60	0	1	0	0	0	355.332	6.297	361,629	686,036
13	61	0	1	0	0	0	389.149	4,723	393,872	686,036
14	62	0	1	0	0	0	426.161	3.148	429,309	686,036
15	63	0	1	0	0	0	466.750	1.574	468,324	686,036
16	64	0	1	0	0	0	510.813	0	510.813	686,036
17	65	0	1	0	65,348	-65,348	487.926	0	557,817	616,145
18	66	0	1	0	65,348	-65,348	465.147	0	609,788	581,007
19	67	0	1	0	65,348	-65,348	442.182	0	666,769	562,200
20	68	0	1	0	65,348	-65,348	419.100	0	729,192	543,063
				200,000	261,393	-61,393				
21	69	0	1	0	65,348	-65,348	396.032	0	797,572	523,643
22	70	0	1	0	65,348	-65,348	373.130	0	872,476	504,001
23	71	0	1	0	65,348	-65,348	350.576	0	954,528	474,665
24	72	0	1	0	65,348	-65,348	328.807	0	1,044,636	443,717
25	73	0	1	0	65,348	-65,348	308.190	0	1.143,673	411,120

The values and benefits are not guaranteed and are subject to change unless the column is marked guaranteed. This supplemental illustration must be accompanied by a basic illustration for required disclosure.

Now, let's look at some of the inner workings of the EIUL contract. In other words, what happens to the funds on a yearly basis and how does this work to your advantage? <u>Is it actually possible to develop a system that allows the same dollars to work twice for you?</u> Yes! In fact, this concept will be one of your most powerful wealth building tools! (See diagram on page 45, "Make the Same Dollar Work Twice For You")

Table A is for illustration purposes only. It depicts a hypothetical case of the growth potential of funds within the insurance contract for a person beginning at age 41. The contract is funded in five equal, yearly amounts of $50,000 for a total of $250,000.

Table A:

End of Year	Age	Modal Premium	Times Per Year	Annual Premium	Cash From Policy	Annual Outlay	Surr Cash Value	Surr Charge	Account Value	Death Benefit
1	41	50,000	1	50,000	0	50,000	14,529	32,343	46,872	1,271,862
2	42	50,000	1	50,000	0	50,000	67,642	30,187	97,829	1,271,862
3	43	50,000	1	50,000	0	50,000	125,216	28,031	153,247	1,271,862
4	44	50,000	1	50,000	0	50,000	187,612	25,875	213,487	1,271,862
5	45	50,000	1	50,000	0	50,000	255,298	23,719	279,017	1,271,862
6	46	0	1	0	0	0	277,213	21,562	298,775	1,271,862
7	47	0	1	0	0	0	300,821	19,406	320,227	1,271,862
8	48	0	1	0	0	0	326,279	17,250	343,529	1,271,862
9	49	0	1	0	0	0	353,758	15,094	368,852	1,271,862
10	50	0	1	0	0	0	387,289	12,937	400,226	1,271,862
				250,000	0	250,000				
11	51	0	1	0	0	0	426,148	10,781	436,929	1,271,862
12	52	0	1	0	0	0	468,612	8,625	477,237	1,271,862
13	53	0	1	0	0	0	515,073	6,469	521,541	1,271,862
14	54	0	1	0	0	0	565,867	4,312	570,179	1,271,862
15	55	0	1	0	0	0	621,479	2,156	623,635	1,271,862
16	56	0	1	0	0	0	682,182	0	682,182	1,271,862
17	57	0	1	0	0	0	746,576	0	746,576	1,271,862
18	58	0	1	0	0	0	817,424	0	817,424	1,271,862
19	59	0	1	0	0	0	895,409	0	895,409	1,271,862
20	60	0	1	0	0	0	981,285	0	981,285	1,275,671
				250,000	0	250,000				

Note! The primary objective of using an EIUL contract is to assist in cash accumulation. However, there are other benefits that you gain in the process. One obvious benefit is that you instantly create a tax-free estate that is passed on to your heirs in the event of your premature death. Your contract is purposely structured as part of a long-term plan. With this in mind, you will see in later years, cost of the death benefit coverage is almost non existent.

Refer to Table A, above. At the end of year five, the account value is estimated to be approximately $279,000. Up until year five, excess funds were always available for other high-yield investments. So, after year five, how do you continue to invest in future high-yield investments if all the excess funds are being used to fund the EIUL contract? According to the terms of your contract, you have the ability to borrow funds from the policy in an amount slightly lower than the actual Surrender Cash Value. This is the most exciting aspect of using the EIUL contract to create wealth. There are no limitations on the use of the funds and the amount of time required to access the funds is minimal; usually the funds can be accessed via a telephone call and a wire transfer. In almost all situations, accessing your funds does not involve any transaction fees.

Looking closer at the Surrender Cash Value, in the illustration above, you see you can begin borrowing from the policy as early as year two.

It is extremely important you understand the following two statements with regard to borrowing from your EIUL contract. Once you do, you will understand why this process is so effective in assisting you to grow your long-term investment portfolio.

1. Interest charged on the borrowed funds is lower than the projected interest amount credited to your Account Value on an annual basis.
2. Interest credited to the Account Value is calculated as though no loan had ever been taken from the policy.

These two aspects of the policy create a unique opportunity to increase your investment performance; all with no additional effort on your part. Let's analyze exactly what is happening in the process.

- You are able to earn a higher interest rate on the Account Value and pay a lower rate on the borrowed funds. This creates arbitrage!
- Funds continue to grow tax-free within the policy.
- Funds are not restricted to use. (Available for other high yield investments.)
- No fees are charged for accessing funds.
- Death Benefit minus borrowed funds, remain intact.

<u>At first, many of our clients look at this plan in complete disbelief</u>! Most of them wonder why anyone would not want to start a plan like this. Here is where we usually separate the doers from the non-doers!

Without question, the most significant factors involved with someone starting a plan, is the fact that the plan…

- Is long-term
- Needs to be treated like a business
- Requires **<u>discipline</u>** to stick to the plan

Once you are ready to commit to this proven process, like our other clients, you will realize this system works very well. It will work equally as well for you. Congratulations! You are almost ready to get started.

Before we continue, let us emphasize, your entire strategy should be geared to creating wealth, establishing a plan that provides tax-free retirement income and if needed, establish a source of emergency funds. In order to meet your long-term goals, we cannot over emphasize that every time you withdraw funds from your policy **<u>prior</u>** to retirement, you will need to replace the funds along with the interest. We will discuss this in more detail in the chapter titled, "Becoming Your Own Banker."

<u>Now it's time to reveal the most unique aspect of why the EIUL contract is the perfect tool for your financial plan.</u> <u>We have intentionally saved the best for last!</u>

This sounds terrific, but how do you receive your retirement funds, completely tax-free? Due to the provisions of TAMRA, TEFRA and DEFRA, you are allowed to access your funds at the time of retirement by withdrawing the funds via policy loans. Repayment of the loans is not required and the loan proceeds from the policy are completely tax-free. An Equity Indexed Universal Life product is a financial tool that allows your funds to compound and grow in a tax-free environment. However, you must use an INVESTMENT GRADE insurance contract to make all of this work for you.

As you begin to borrow from the policy, in yearly increments, the death benefit will decrease. However, earlier we stated, you are not using this contract to provide a death benefit for family survivors. <u>You are using it to accumulate wealth in a tax-free environment and to provide a retirement income that is also tax-free</u>. We assist you in structuring your plan properly and calculating the amount of funds you will require each year. This will ensure you never run out of money and the policy stays in affect until your death. At that time, the remaining death benefit will be distributed (**tax-free**) to your heirs.

So now you know about one of the most valuable investment vehicles used for over a hundred years by the very wealthy! You are ready to get started! Suddenly, it occurs to you that you might not be insurable due to bad health. Don't let this deter you from your plan. There is a provision in all insurance contracts called insurable interest. It allows you to establish your plan via a close relative such as a child, grandchild or spouse.

Let's apply some out-of-the-box thinking and see how to <u>properly</u> fund a college savings plan for your children. You are a young married couple with a two-year old child. Everyone keeps telling you that you should start a college plan for your child and that the best strategy is to begin saving by depositing tax deductible funds into a qualified 529(b) college plan. It seems everyone follows this method. But, is there a different investment vehicle that can work better for you? You bet there is!

Instead, you purchase an EIUL contract for your child. You calculate the amount of funds required at or around the child's age 18. You have limited financial resources, so you decide to fund the policy over a period of 16 years. This works extremely well and we recommend that you begin a plan as early as possible. As you can see, the child in the example below is age 2.

Designed for: College Bound — $915,091 Selected Face Amount
Issue Age: 2 — Initial Annual Premium: $3,600.00
Female, Standard — Initial Death Benefit Option: Level

Supplemental Report Description: This report shows both the account value and cash surrender value, and lists the schedule of surrender charges for the illustrated policy.

							Non-Guaranteed Assumed			
End of Year	Age	Modal Premium	Times Per Year	Annual Premium	Cash From Policy	Annual Outlay	Surr Cash Value	Surr Charge	Account Value	Death Benefit
1	3	3,600	1	3,600	0	3,600	0	4,593	2,332	915,091
2	4	3,600	1	3,600	0	3,600	645	4,287	4,932	915,091
3	5	3,600	1	3,600	0	3,600	3,797	3,981	7,777	915,091
4	6	3,600	1	3,600	0	3,600	7,216	3,674	10,890	915,091
5	7	3,600	1	3,600	0	3,600	10,918	3,368	14,287	915,091
6	8	3,600	1	3,600	0	3,600	14,901	3,062	17,963	915,091
7	9	3,600	1	3,600	0	3,600	19,218	2,756	21,974	915,091
8	10	3,600	1	3,600	0	3,600	23,902	2,450	26,352	915,091
9	11	3,600	1	3,600	0	3,600	28,976	2,143	31,120	915,091
10	12	3,600	1	3,600	0	3,600	34,723	1,837	36,560	915,091
				36,000	0	36,000				
11	13	3,600	1	3,600	0	3,600	41,539	1,531	43,070	915,091
12	14	3,600	1	3,600	0	3,600	48,997	1,225	50,222	915,091
13	15	3,600	1	3,600	0	3,600	57,164	919	58,082	915,091
14	16	3,600	1	3,600	0	3,600	66,108	612	66,721	915,091
15	17	3,600	1	3,600	0	3,600	75,910	306	76,216	915,091
16	18	3,600	1	3,600	0	3,600	86,645	0	86,645	915,091
17	19	0	1	0	0	0	94,372	0	94,372	915,091
18	20	0	1	0	0	0	102,846	0	102,846	915,091
19	21	0	1	0	0	0	112,156	0	112,156	915,091
20	22	0	1	0	0	0	122,375	0	122,375	915,091
				57,600	0	57,600				

The values and benefits are not guaranteed and are subject to change unless the column is marked guaranteed.
This supplemental illustration must be accompanied by a basic illustration for required disclosure.

By the time the child reaches age 18, there is $86,645 available for college tuition or whatever venture you choose to help your child to accomplish.

However, let us suggest an alternative for funding the policy. This situation may be applicable to you. Many of our clients have parents who are part of the "Baby Boomer" generation. Their parents have exceeded their financial expectations and would like to participate in setting aside funds for their grandchildren's college education. They review their grandchildren's college funding needs and, since they understand the power of larger lump sum investing, they decide to gift five, yearly investments to each grandchild. The grandparents receive a tax deduction for the gifts and the parents have peace of mind knowing that their children's education will be funded in advance.

Why is this better than a traditional 529(b) college plan? Let's summarize the benefits!

- Amount of funds deposited are not limited
- Use of funds is not restricted to use for college tuition only
- Your child begins an EIUL plan that can continue to grow after college is completed
- If your child does not attend college, the funds are not heavily penalized and taxed
- Principal is not at risk
- Higher tax-free earnings on funds within the policy
- Funds can be borrowed from the EIUL contract, to make a down payment on home or business venture without paying penalties or taxes
- Death benefit is provided in case of a premature death of the child
- Parents own and control the policy during college saving years, yet policy can be transferred to child at any time
- Cash value of policy is not considered when applying for financial aid or a scholarship

The last item listed is a huge benefit. Most people are not aware that the cash value within a life insurance contract is not taken into consideration when calculating the assets of a person applying for financial aid. This is a great example of how you might consider using an EIUL contract.

Occasionally, our younger clients are hesitant to start a plan because they recognize while their finances will improve over time, they are, currently, limited in their ability to save. We advise them that while they cannot 'increase' the size of a plan they have already put in place; they can always start another plan at a later date. So, don't put off starting a plan just because it is not as large as you feel it should be from day one.

Note: Stocks or mutual funds are susceptible to losses within the market, so investors are vulnerable to principal losses. Principal protection is a significant benefit to utilizing an EIUL contract. Once the interest earnings have been credited to the account, the Account Value can never drop below that amount. It is guaranteed! The interest earnings become part of the principal going forward. In Table A, on page 40, the Account Value illustrates the projected amount of the principal balance with interest added each year.

BECOMING YOUR OWN BANKER

How would you like to establish, fund and manage your own Personal Banking System? In other words, become your own bank! Perhaps the most exciting aspect of setting up your Equity Indexed Universal Life policy to supercharge your wealth is the concept of Becoming Your Own Banker. How would you like to know that one day, in the near future, you will never again pay finance fees on any unsecured lines of credit (credit cards) or a major purchase such as an automobile? By becoming your own banker and borrowing from yourself you will amass wealth more quickly.

There are a number of opportunities for you to make loans, to yourself, from your bank. Consider large ticket items such as a house, a boat or home remodeling costs. In this particular situation you could expect to…

- Create arbitrage on the borrowed funds or earn 1 to 3% on funds that still are working in your policy for you.
- Recapture all of the principal and interest you would have paid to a finance company as you repay these short-term loans.

Another way to use your bank would be to make loans to family members. Perhaps your daughter or son or grandchildren are considering purchasing their first home. In this scenario you could expect to…

- Earn arbitrage on the funds borrowed from the policy at the rate of 1-3%.
- Earn a rate of return from the loan you extended to the family member.
- Take an equity interest in the home you assist in financing, if you desire.

How about assisting your children or grandchildren or a beloved niece or nephew with their college education?

The third method is the most exciting way to become your own banker. This method helps you explode your wealth, once you have your banking system in place and have it funded. In this scenario, you take short-term loans for investment purposes. Remember, we would not have you risk your capital unless the returns on the outside of the fund were either contractually guaranteed or principal protected; so invest with confidence.

The section titled "The Most Overlooked Investment Tool," introduced Equity Indexed Universal Life as the foundation of your long-term financial plan. That section referenced this chapter and how you would utilize your life insurance contract to become your own banker. Regardless of how you fund your contract, you will see that the Account Value continues to increase on an annual basis. The funds in the Cash Surrender Value column are available to you once they have been credited to the policy. You have the ability to borrow the funds at a rate that is lower than (typically 1-3%) the rate that is being credited to your Account Value. The Account Value continues to be credited as though no loan was ever taken out. With this in mind, you are now creating arbitrage within the policy itself.

In our previous example, we referenced an individual who funded an EIUL contract with five equal contributions of $50,000 for a total of $250,000. Let's assume this is your policy and you borrow against it to make a purchase such as a new car. The new vehicle is going to cost $30,000. You take out a policy loan for a period of four years and make monthly payments back to your policy. The only difference in this transaction is that you are paying yourself, instead of paying non-deductible interest to a bank or finance company. You were going to purchase the vehicle anyway, so why shouldn't you be the one to make a profit on this transaction. After all, it is your hard earned money and you deserve the reward! At the end of four years, the car is paid in full, the policy loan is paid in full and you have gained the value of the car after four years of depreciation. If that value is 50% of original value, you have gained a net profit of $15,000. Remember, when applying the principles in this book, to view your entire plan as though you are managing a profitable business. In this transaction, you became your own banker and made a profit of $15,000. That equates to an annual return of approximately 12.5% on an investment of $30,000 which is already earning 1%-3% arbitrage within the policy itself! Your funds are now working twice for you!

The most fantastic aspect of this car purchase is that you were able to purchase a depreciating asset and yet, in the end, you created additional wealth for yourself. What would happen if you were able to purchase an appreciating asset such as real estate? In this situation, you could expect to borrow various sums and put them to work for you in real estate deals. When you only have to come up with 10% of the property value, or in some cases much less, you can put your money to work for you over and over again in relatively short periods of time. This subject will be discussed in more detail in the chapter dealing with leverage.

You may have the opportunity to invest in other business ventures in the coming years. It's your money. You decide how you want to invest it. Following is a diagram that should help you understand how this all works.

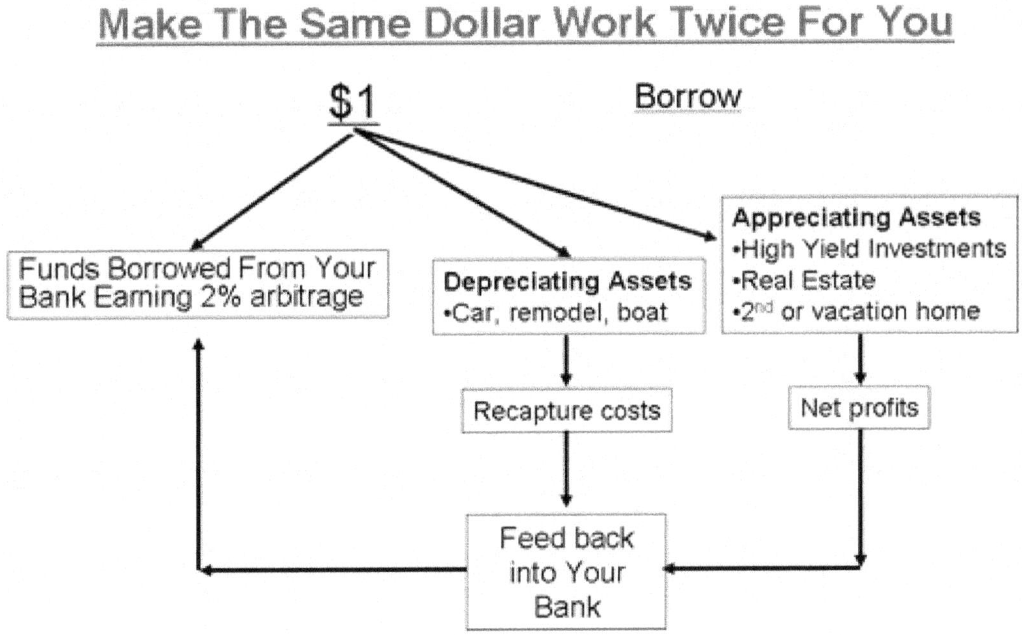

However you choose to invest, we recommend that you apply the same investment standards to your outside investments as you do to your investment in an Equity Indexed Life Insurance contract. Be certain that any investment you choose meets the following criteria:

- Is the principal safe?
- Are your funds liquid?
- Does the investment provide a rate of return commensurate with the risk?
- Are there any tax benefits, associated with the investment?

If you have ever wondered why there is a bank on nearly every street corner, perhaps now, you understand why! It is possible to become extremely wealthy earning, what would appear to be, very small rates of return (such as 1%-3%). This is an advanced concept as it allows you to put the same dollar to work twice for you. First, you earn 1%-3% on the money in the first layer from the arbitrage you create within your life insurance contract. Next, during the same time frame, you earn a higher rate of return on the same dollars borrowed from your contract when you invest in high yield investments.

Now you have the knowledge and the proper investment vehicle to become your own banker so that you can earn the profits that the banks have earned for centuries!

THE STOCK MARKET AND MUTUAL FUNDS

There have been countless numbers of books written about the stock market. And, in recent years, with the explosion of the masses migrating towards day trading, there have been many books written that cover the technical aspect of trading. That being said, the authors want to note that this chapter will be devoted solely to the discussion of the stock market and the risks associated with investing in individual stocks and mutual funds over the long-term as <u>a major portion</u> of one's retirement planning portfolio.

How long has the stock market been around?

Wall Street can trace its name back to 1653. Originally it was set up for defense and not for commerce. Settlers of Dutch descent and the British built a 12 foot stockade fence. Little did they know that this fence would go on to become the center of financial activity in the world! The wall lasted until 1685. At that point, the wall was torn down and a new street was built. The British called it Wall Street. The emergence of two great Stock Exchanges helped Wall Street rise to pre-eminence? The Exchanges gave order to the chaotic trading and gave rise to the financial markets as we know them today. Suffice it to say, Wall Street and the concept of "The Markets" has been around for a very long time.

The authors believe that due to the long, rich history of the Stock Market, many people tend to entrust their investments without question or proper due diligence. In other words, people equate the tradition associated with the stock market to the idea of safety of principal. The widely promoted method of 'buy and hold' investing gives most investors a false sense of security. The media tells us that if you invest in and hold onto a position long enough, you will be richly rewarded for enduring the down years; where principal was lost and gains were no where in sight. Since 2000, many investors in the NASDAQ market understand that when you lose 60% or more of your portfolio, it is likely gone for good. That index is still down close to 50% after nearly 7 years.

With the advent of internet and trading online, the market cycles have increased in pace relative to pre-computer trading. Buy and hold is certainly still a viable strategy, but the buy and hold period has become drastically reduced. The fast pace of information exchange has actually reduced the cycle time for many new stocks. This has created many millionaires, in recent years and has also stumped investors who are the product of earlier market cycles. Unfortunately, those stumped investors are the same ones who have been fooled by the buy and hold strategy and have lost thousands upon thousands of dollars. Refer to 1987 and 2000 market crashes.

The Dow 30…It's not what you think it is

The Dow 30 (Dow Jones Industrial Average) is the most widely recognized stock market indicator in the United States. All 30 stocks are listed on the New York Stock Exchange (NYSE). These are blue chip companies that reflect the health of the U.S. economy.

Have you ever seen a chart of the Dow 30 from 1900 to present? It is simply amazing! The chart is illustrated showing an undeniable progression upwards – a beautiful 45 degree angle of ascent; a sign of solid strength in any index. What most people do not realize is the fact that since its inception, in 1928, the Dow 30 has been comprised of many more stocks than the original 30 with which it began. What does this mean to such a chart or graphical illustration of an index?

Allow us to digress for a moment. If we were to tell you that we knew of a car engine that got unlimited miles to the gallon of gas. You would be very interested in how that is possible. We would, of course, tell you we used the same model of car throughout the measurement. What if we failed to tell you that each morning, we got into a brand new car with a full tank of gas. In other words, the tank never ran out!

The Dow 30 graphs are much like this very flawed gas mileage analogy. The principals at the stock exchange consistently put in a brand new strong stocks and cull out the dead wood or non-performing equities. Over time, the index appears to be an unstoppable machine that always produces fantastic returns; if one is willing to wait long enough. Referring back to the car - we did not tell you we started with a brand new car and a full tank of gas every morning of measurement – a sad omission of facts. Similarly, no one rushes to tell the general public that out of the original Dow 30 stocks only 2 stocks from 1928 are still a part of the index. By the way, these remaining two stocks are no where near their all time highs, either. So what happened to all of those stocks that were once a part of the almighty Dow 30? Many, of the original Dow 30, have become de-listed. A stock is de-listed when it violates one or more exchange rules, which then causes it to be removed from the exchange (and the index.) At the same time the weak stock was removed from the exchange, it was replaced with a brand new company stock that was just beginning to 'run up'; hence the appearance of strength over time.

The Dow: 1900 through the Present

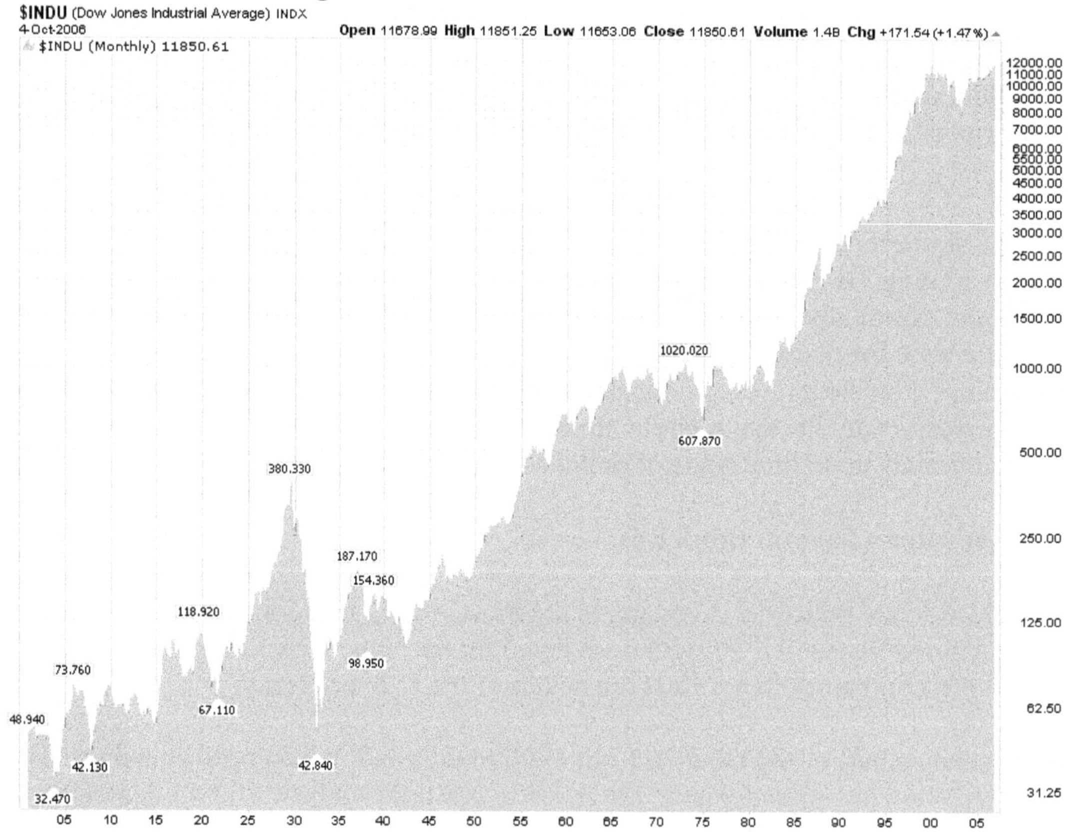

Mutual Funds

Although the popularity of mutual funds has risen dramatically in recent decades, they are by no means a brand new concept. At the turn of this century, the number of mutual funds exceeded the number of individual stocks trading at any one time. This has been the case for many years. In fact, there are so many mutual funds in existence now you can even purchase mutual funds comprised of other mutual funds.

While mutual funds do provide liquidity, and unique diversification possibilities, they come with tremendous risk. As there is no downside protection, or principal protection, one can suffer substantial losses in their portfolio. There is no way to hedge your positions in mutual funds, (with stocks you can use options to hedge against losses). There is no ability to protect yourself and you also pay very heavy management fees, whether or not you have any performance gains. You are essentially being penalized twice in your investing account, once for poor performance of the fund and a second time for the privilege of being a part of the fund that lost your principal. It is not a sound business practice to invest the majority of your portfolio in this manner.

If you have a typical, company sponsored 401(k) plan, you are generally offered a 'basket' of mutual funds in which to invest. The only individual stock offered in these 401(k) plans, is usually that of the company sponsoring the plan. If you maintain your own IRA, perhaps one containing funds from a former employer, you are usually limited to investing in mutual funds or fixed interest funds.

The authors do not recommend investing in any instrument that does not offer principal protection. We cannot endorse investing solely in mutual funds as a prudent means of long-term planning. If you must invest in mutual funds, invest in a fund that is 'indexed' or tracks the major indexes (Dow, NASDAQ or SP500). Also, only invest a portion of your portfolio in the stock market. Regardless of how you decide to invest, please remember you are subjecting yourself to heavy fees unnecessarily when you invest in mutual funds.

A better alternative, with the same performance potential and substantially lower fees, would be to invest in Exchange Traded Funds (ETFs). Of course, there are many ETFs that track the major indexes for you to choose from. They are superior to mutual funds in many ways. Educate yourself on their merits and drawbacks or seek competent investment advice before you invest your hard earned dollars.

Corruption in the Markets

Another sad aspect to what should be a fantastic place to invest is corruption in the markets. The natural state of the markets provides a relatively safe, predictable place to invest over time. With all of the corruption in individual company stocks and mutual fund trading practices, the markets are a treacherous place to venture into; unless you have downside protection. As you recall, hedging against losses in the markets is not easy to do; particularly not in mutual funds.

Could there be another Enron or WorldCom fiasco – you bet there could! Instead of dwelling upon these negative events, we recommend that you become pro-active in your retirement business and eliminate the possibility of becoming a victim to any future illegal business practices of this nature. Seek to protect principal wherever possible. More importantly, seek to contract for your expected investment gains.

But the Stock Market is so glamorous!

Yes, it is glamorous. Many people have done very well to invest their hard earned money over time. If you desire to trade your accounts as a part of your financial planning, we would only advise that you go through proper training in stock investing before putting up any real cash. Unfortunately, with the way our 401(k) plans are structured, many people are forced into making decisions about their investments without any market education from which to draw. Stock and Mutual Fund Trading requires tremendous discipline. We will agree that there are those traders that do exceedingly well. Just like any discipline, there are the superstars and then, there are those that lose. Trading in any form, for that matter, is not for everyone. There are many safer ways for you to grow your portfolio.

The Baby Boomers and the Stock Market

The Baby Boomers have been responsible for waves of spending which in turn boosted our economy at various points throughout recent history – really since World War II.
Author, Harry S. Dent Jr., has written extensively about cycles in demographics and illustrates, for us, the tremendous power that, this group of individuals wield. They have the power to stimulate and disintegrate!

Historically, the Japanese stock market precedes the US Stock Market in terms of performance. In Japan, during the early 1990's, the Japanese government decided to raise interest rates in a very inflated environment. The decision caused the Nikkei Stock Index to crash 30,000 points from its high of 40,000 points. Since that shattering event, their market has not ever returned to its former highs. Harry S. Dent, Jr., reminds us that, yes, history does repeat itself in his book The Next Great Bubble Boom. He tells us how our market parallels that of the Japanese, but also many of the demographics that caused the crash are in play in our markets, approximately ten years behind.

So how can you protect yourself?

- Invest the majority of your portfolio in principal protected products.
- Use asset class diversification to avoid investing too heavily in the stock market.
- Invest only 20% to 30% of your overall funds in this class.
- Use products that are indexed to the markets, but do not necessarily have your funds working directly in the marketplace. (Note! Equity Indexed Universal Life works perfectly.)

Our recommended method of investing allows you to safely invest your money, earn a high rate of return and still sleep at night; all without taking on the responsibility and stress of personally trading your investment accounts.

HIGH YIELD INVESTMENTS

Your Hedge Against Inflation

No discussion of yield on dollars invested (or rate of return) would be complete without first establishing a benchmark. We shall use inflation as that benchmark. Below, we discuss its ability to erode your purchasing power like a silent thief. Next, we demonstrate the Rule of 72 and how you should use it to ensure that your savings will allow you to maintain your current lifestyle and/or improve it in retirement. Then, we show you the necessity of investing in high yield investments to ensure your retirement planning success.

CPI and the True Rate of Inflation

The CPI, or Consumer Price Index, is widely used as an indicator of the change in the general level of consumer prices or the rate of inflation. Since the purchasing power of money is affected by changes in prices, the CPI *can be* useful to Consumers. American consumers can compare movements in the CPI to changes in their personal income to monitor and evaluate changes in their financial situation.

The CPI is generally used to escalate a given dollar value over time to preserve the purchasing power of that value. Thus the CPI is used widely to adjust contracted payments such as wages, rents, leases and child or spousal support allowances.

You, like many other consumers, may not be aware of the fact that the CPI is calculated without factoring in food or fuel costs! The government tells us that these two price factors are too volatile to include! Besides, few of us actually eat and drive, right? Unfortunately, leaving out these two numbers renders the CPI value that is reported on a monthly basis virtually useless in determining the true rate of inflation. Some macro-economists tell us that with food and fuel calculated into the formula, the true rate of inflation is actually closer to 5% or higher! That is a far cry from the 3.1% that the CPI typically hovers near, according to government reports.

Just this small piece of misinformation can have disastrous effects upon your retirement planning as we show you below in the "Rule of 72" section. The true rate of inflation is eroding your buying power at an alarming pace; failing to account for it, could cause you to fail in reaching your retirement goals.

Rule of 72

Have you ever heard of the Rule of 72? If you have, you know that it is a critical component of investment planning. Dividing the number 72 by the expected Rate of Return (ROR) on an investment determines how many years it will take for your original investment to double. Conversely, by dividing the number of years available for doubling your money into 72, you can identify the rate of return necessary to accomplish your goal. The Rule of 72 also shows us how quickly we need to double our investments in order to keep pace with inflation. We have provided a few calculations of this powerful concept below for your reference. (Remember! The columns are interchangeable in determining either rate of return or time necessary to double your money.)

Rate Of Return	Years To Double
5%	14.4
10%	7.2
12%	6.0
22%	3.3
24%	3.0
30%	2.4

If you recall, we mentioned that some of the foremost macro economists in our country today are calculating the true pace of inflation at 5% per year. Using the Rule of 72 we divide 72 by 5 and come up with a doubling period of 14.4 years. Let's see how this works by working through an example.

In terms of outpacing inflation, the average wage earner must ensure that every 14.4 years they generate twice the dollars they are using today to maintain the same standard of living. If you already work an 80 hour work week, this is terrible news! If you make $100,000 today and do not do everything possible to ensure that you are earning $200,000 per year 14.4 years from now, you will have to cut your standard of living drastically. Sadly, if you were still earning $100,000, 14.4 years from now, your purchasing power would simply erode by 50%! There is something you can do about it though! Seek investments that outpace inflation and you will come out ahead. It is a mathematical certainty!

Please note that some individuals might disagree with the 5% figure. In fact you might be one of them. That is OK! This section of our book is not intended to create an argument one way or another. However, based upon historical data and current prices of consumer goods, we do believe that the true rate of inflation is actually above 5%. If you choose to plan your investments using 6%-7% inflation as your benchmark, you will never get behind in your savings goals.

Higher Rates of Return are not a Luxury, They are a Necessity!

Now that you understand your purchasing power is not eroding at the pace of 3.1% as reported, but closer to 5% per year, you must realize it is extremely important to place your investment dollars carefully. Higher rates of return are not simply a luxury; they are a necessity to maintaining your lifestyle going forward. But, you tell us, you want a better lifestyle in retirement; well, then you need to be ever more vigilant in your placement of those dollars and the velocity at which you double your money.

It is an interesting calculation to see what kind of action you need to take, <u>now</u>, in your planning to ensure you do <u>not</u> need to cut your standard of living in the coming years or in retirement.

Let's run the numbers. We have an individual, Robert, who is currently age 45 who plans to retire by age 65. Robert has 20 years to really pull his retirement dollars together into an effective plan that will sustain him going forward.

Let's assume a 15% annual return on his money outside of the Insurance Plan. Note: At this pace, calculating a 30% income tax bracket, Robert will be able to double his money approximately every 7.0 years. Not bad! Let's now assume he has $100,000 to put to work. Doubling the initial $100,000 approximately 3 times (remember 20/7.0 = 2.8 doubling periods), will earn him approximately $800,000.00 over that 20 year time frame.

Let's be conservative and use 5% inflation for this example. If Robert lives on $50,000 per year today, he will need $85,000 per year in 10 years, $146,000 per year in 20 years and $200,000 per year in about 30 years. As long as he continues to earn 15% per year, consistently, his plan will work very well. By taking action now, Robert has hedged against inflation and removed the potential penalties of Opportunity Costs and Procrastination. If Robert decided not to take action and instead left that $100,000 in a CD earning about 5% per year, barring any financial emergencies, he would have about $281,000 or slightly less than 2 years worth of living expenses set aside 20 years from now. That will not take him very far in terms of living comfortably in retirement. If he were to sustain <u>any</u> financial emergencies, his savings and his retirement plans could be wiped out!

Please realize that planning for your future is not a luxury and neither is investing in higher yield investments as do the wealthy. Outpacing inflation and principal protection should be your top two priorities in deciding where to place your investment dollars.

We Live in a Global Economy

The advent of the computer has not only quickened the pace of commerce, it has brought the ability to transact with foreign companies to our desktops! Large companies, small business owners and stay at home parents can run export businesses right from their homes. There is no need to travel outside of the United States to make money by trading goods with people of other nations! This new global economy is prompting an evolution in our stock market, our currencies and our investment decisions. ***Alan Greenspan tells us that it is not prudent to hold our savings in one currency (See Reuters 12/11/2006 Article –"Greenspan says expect more dollar weakness".)***

What are Retail Level Investments?

Mainstream investments – CDs, bonds, mutual funds, money market accounts – these are packaged for the masses – or better known as Retail Investors. Retail Investors represent the last layer of investors that trade investment dollars for a rate of return over time. They receive the lowest rate of return on their dollars invested. You may have heard the phrase – "Don't pay retail, if you don't have to". Investing at the 'retail level' will not serve you well either.

What is an Accredited Investor?

The definition of an Accredited Investor is: A person whose individual net worth or joint net worth with that person's spouse exceeds $1,000,000. A person who had individual income in excess of $200,000 in each of the two most recent years or joint income with that person's spouse in excess of $300,000 in each of those years.

This is the standard that hedge funds (private high-yield funds) require their investors to attain before they will extend and invitation to invest in their high yield funds. Did we mention that hedge funds don't have much downside protection! Even if you had the money to invest in these high level funds, we would not recommend it, because there is no principal protection.

What are Institutional Level Investments?

Institutional level investing is where the larger financial institutions do their investing. These are Fortune 500 companies, more typically Banks and Financial Institutions. Companies like Dell and Bank of America, and John Henry, owner of the Boston Red Sox often times make more money in their investment activities than they do in their regular businesses. These institutions have the capital to invest in these higher yield forms of investments. Typical investments require minimum outlay of tens-of-millions of dollars. Accredited investors are likely to be invited to invest in institutional level deals. The typical Retail Investor has no chance to participate in these deals, unless they are able to pool their money with other Retail Investors or team up with an Accredited or Institutional level investor.

Accredited investors, institutional level investors and this nation's ultra-wealthy are commonly referred to on Wall Street as "Smart Money". Simply stated, Smart Money, knows when, how and where to invest their money for the safest and fastest returns available at any given time.

At Wealth2020, Inc., we recognize the importance of identifying and implementing high yield investment strategies into our client's wealth building program. Our network allows you access to investment products formerly only available to the ultra-wealthy, accredited investors and institutional level investors. When you follow our investment strategies you instantly graduate to this class of investors; you become Smart Money.

OPPORTUNITY COSTS

Opportunity Costs are costs associated with choosing one path over another. In business and life, an opportunity cost can be defined as: Loss of time, earnings, effort or progress due to poor investment decisions or failure to take action in executing an investment plan. The most recognizable opportunity costs in business are the following:

- Choosing To Pay Cash For A High Ticket Purchase versus Using Leverage
- Failure To Execute A Plan of Action in Investing - Procrastination

Let's look at an example of using leverage versus paying cash for a high ticket item.

Oddly enough, paying cash for a new car is one of the poorest investment decisions an individual can make, especially if your financial plan is structured to increase wealth as quickly as possible. If you paid cash to purchase a brand new $30,000 vehicle your opportunity cost would be the interest you could have earned on the $30,000. You might not view the earnings loss as a very big consequence, if you only consider the paltry returns the bank allows us. I agree, 3%-5% returns do not present that big of a threat. For instance, if you were able to earn 5% per year on a CD, you would have an opportunity cost of $1,500.00, minus the cost of financing for the vehicle. However, if you had the opportunity to earn 15% on the money, the opportunity costs start to increase. In this case, the opportunity cost would be $4,500 per year minus the cost of financing.

As you learn to leverage your funds for higher returns the opportunity costs become much greater. It becomes extremely important to weigh your options each time you plan to use your hard earned cash for purchases. For instance, if you were presented with an opportunity to purchase a piece of real estate priced at $100,000 and only needed to put 10%, ($10,000), as a down payment and you knew that your Rate of Return on that investment was going to be $5,000 or 50%, you would have an opportunity cost of $5,000. If you elected to purchase 3 parcels of real estate, putting 10% or $10,000 on each, you could earn $15,000 over the course of the year. Referring back to paying cash for the car, in just two years the earnings from your real estate investments would have accumulated enough funds to pay for the car.

When you learn how to leverage your cash and how to effectively allocate your dollars, you can make the same dollars work twice for you. Please refer back to the section on Arbitrage to understand this concept completely. It is important to note that we recommend becoming your own banker for any cash transaction you plan to make, especially large cash purchases.

The second and often times, most significant opportunity cost, comes disguised as a failure to take action; more commonly known as Procrastination. Waiting to take action on an investment can lead to opportunity costs. Let's say that you had $10,000 to invest and someone presented you with an opportunity to earn $5,000 within one year. Instead you adopted a wait and see approach, you would have essentially lost $5,000 in passive income. The un-earned $5,000 also represents an opportunity cost. Opportunity Costs = Lost Opportunities to increase your net worth.

One of the greatest opportunity costs we face is not recognizing the value of continuing education. When you stop learning you will likely impact your earnings. You paid for this book and probably questioned its price. However the price of the book is insignificant to the value derived if you properly apply the concepts developing your financial plan.

Raleigh and I purchase many e-books that are priced equal to or more than this one. Almost always, we find that the information was worth thousands more than the cost of the book.

For example! In 2006, my wife and I purchased a book **(31 Days to Profits in Probate Real Estate** – By Ron Mead the Probate Guy) for $59.95. This book deals with the subject of purchasing properties in probate. The amazing part about the book is that it is very short. We had been told that a person needed to attend seminars that could cost as much as $3,000 - $5,000 to learn the same material. We used the information to purchase a property with no money down and sold it 30 days later for a net profit of $10,000. Without the information in that book, we would not have known how to complete the transaction without any money out of pocket. Was the book, dealing with probate properties, worth its price? Oh yes! The moral of this story! Do not let the lack of knowledge be one of your most expensive opportunity costs!

THE POWER OF LEVERAGE

"The Power of Leverage" is one of our most exciting chapters. It is purposely placed near the end of our book because the subject matter is most inspiring and it ties all the previous chapters together. Armed with the previous information you should now be better conditioned to the concept of out-of-the-box type thinking and be prepared for some exciting new ideas!

I believe that it was Victor Hugo who stated, "NOTHING CAN STOP AN IDEA WHOSE TIME HAS COME!" That statement has never been more applicable, than it is today! <u>The time has come</u> for the ideas in this book!

During the mid to late 90's, real estate in many segments of the US was booming. It was not uncommon to see property values increasing by percentages in the double digit ranges from 10% to as high as 50% per year. Many investors made tremendous profits by purchasing properties and flipping them one or two years later. Other investors, who had the foresight to purchase properties during the down markets of the late 80's and early 90's, were able to sell their properties with large gains in value.

Based upon extensive research dating back to the 1940's, there are many real estate investors who believe that market conditions are perfect for replicating the same profit-making-opportunities that existed in the mid to late 90's. Raleigh and I agree! Markets are cyclical and the real estate market is no exception to the rule.

Although a few markets in the US have been strong from 2001 through 2005, most markets have seen considerable depreciation or have stayed relatively flat. Buy low-sell high has always been the mantra of savvy investors. Markets fit basically into two categories. Buy and sell for quick profits in a highly appreciating market or buy and hold for a slowly appreciating market. Either market has the ability to produce high returns. The end of 2006 and beginning of 2007 present a tremendous profit potential for the investor who understands the buy and hold strategy.

Think about it! Regardless of highly advertised foreclosure rates, families still need a place to live. Rental properties will become more in demand and rental rates will increase. This is another cycle that has repeated itself from the early 1940's.

Investing in real estate is unique. It is not like other investments that require a dollar for dollar outlay, similar to that of purchasing stocks or annuities. Most real estate purchases usually require a maximum down payment of 20%, but down payments can be as little as 5%. Within the last five years, new mortgage products have been introduced that are very investor friendly. That means the traditional guidelines requiring higher down payments have become more lenient.

With this in mind, high yield investment opportunities in real estate become more attractive to the seasoned investor. But what if you are not a seasoned investor? How does this work to your advantage? Don't worry! We will address this issue later in the chapter!

Unlike investing in the stock market, real estate is an investment that is actually secured by something of value. The thing of value is the real property that is being purchased. The property has an appraised value based upon comparisons of other, like properties in the surrounding market.

How does the subject of LEVERAGE apply to real estate? In order to answer this question it is best to look at an example of an actual real estate transaction.

Mary Smith owned a single family rental home. It was free and clear of any mortgage payments and needed very little updating. Mary wanted to get out of the rental business and decided to sell the house. An investor approached her with an offer to purchase the house for investment purposes with the following terms.

Appraised Value	$220,000
Purchase price	$175,000
Down payment	5,000
Owner carry financing	170,000
Balloon payment for full balance, 5 yrs	
Interest only payment 5.5%	
Monthly interest payment	779
Monthly taxes	113
Monthly insurance	80
Total Monthly Payment	$972

This house was resold to a Tenant/Buyer under the terms of a lease option contract.

New sales price	$225,000
Lease/Option down payment	5,000
Monthly lease payments	1,200
Term of the agreement, 4 yrs	
Tenant/Buyer <u>responsible for all maintenance and repairs</u>	

At this point, don't try to analyze the terms or conditions of the property purchase. You just need to know that this was a real purchase that produced the stated numbers.

This transaction shows a positive cash flow of approximately $225 per month or $2700 per year. If you calculate the Return on Investment (ROI) for the $5,000 it is 54% per year for a period of 4 years. More importantly, the sales price of $225,000 minus the purchase price of 175,000 yields an additional profit of $50,000 less closing costs at the end of 4 years. The 4 year ROI is approximately 1216% or 304% per year.

This example depicts the power of leverage at its finest. With a small $5,000 down payment, the investor was able to purchase a home valued at $220,000 and secure financing without a traditional bank credit report. For those of you who really analyzed this transaction, you already figured out that the actual return on investment is <u>infinite</u> because the $5,000 deposit was returned by the tenant/buyer at the time of the lease/option contract. However, the investor did not calculate that aspect of the transaction at the time of the original purchase of the property.

How do we know the exact details of this transaction? I (Jerry) purchased and sold this home in the early stages of our real estate investment career. It is one of many similar transactions that would follow in the upcoming years.

Real estate investment opportunities present themselves in many different forms and transaction types. The transaction in this example is not one that is readily available without a bit of time and effort to find it. The actual time required to find this property took only about 30 days. The time required to find a qualified Tenant/Buyer for the property took approximately 60 days. The purpose of using this transaction in our example is to get you to begin thinking about the possibilities that are available for creating wealth within your plan.

Real Estate investing has a glamorous perception in the eyes of many individuals. Almost any day of the week you can view a late night, television infomercial promoting the get-rich-quick possibilities of investing in real estate.

However, you should be aware that there are risks associated with any type of investment that you pursue and it is our contention that your first rule of investing should be the preservation of principal. Many of our prospects initially ask the question, "Why do I need the EIUL contract if I can make these high rates of returns via real estate investing?"

If you understand the concepts presented throughout the book, you have the advantage of already knowing the answer to that question. The EIUL contract provides the foundation as well as the road-map for you to follow. You already know the end results. The transactions you will fund with your own bank (cash values within the contract), throughout the years of your plan, will vary as different opportunities arise.

Opportunity Costs will not be part of your misfortune, in the future. You will be able to capitalize on opportunities that never seemed possible in the past.

When we introduce these proven concepts to new prospects, we are very explicit about the fact that we are only interested in working with individuals who are committed to success. We are not interested in working with clients who are more interested in what we call, 'the new idea of the month club'! We first develop a solid plan that will serve as the foundation and then add all the other elements that will assist to create wealth much faster.

Both authors (Raleigh and Jerry) are seasoned real estate investors. Real estate is a significant portion of our individual, financial portfolios and with proper due diligence it can also be a significant factor of your wealth creating plan.

As you begin to strategize and plan for your financial future, it is important that you recognize one major reality of investing in real estate. Finding good deals can consume a considerable amount of your time. It also requires common sense and hard work. For this reason, we advise that your entire portfolio should include diversification of various types of safe and sound investments. Real estate will be only one of them.

If you concentrated on finding, only one property per year, that provided the same returns as our example and combined that with other conservative investments yielding 12% - 30% per year, the net results would be astounding. Those along with the growth within the EIUL contract will ensure financial success. Most of all, you will be able to sleep at night, knowing that you are managing your financial future and are in complete control.

In our original outline of investing principles, it was mentioned that we now live in a global economy. This is especially true in the real estate market. Due to the communication capabilities of the internet, it is sometimes just as easy to purchase a property in other states as it is to purchase a property in your own back yard. It is even possible to consider high yield real estate opportunities that are in other countries. With your new found knowledge, keep an open mind to these lucrative opportunities that might be made available to you within the wealth creating years of your plan.

There is one other segment of the real estate market that very few investors understand. We would like to introduce this to you as another idea to add to your new way of thinking.

Discounted real estate notes! What are they?

Every person purchasing a piece of real estate will usually purchase the property with some type of bank or private financing. Many times it is a combination of both. If they did not use a form of financing, all cash would have been required for the purchase.

As stated earlier, home foreclosures within the US are at an all time high. Many foreclosures are purchased by investors by getting the bank to accept a short payoff of the mortgage that is owed by the homeowner. This tactic requires a great amount of knowledge and perseverance on the part of the investor. However, there is another method that the banks sometimes prefer if they decide they are going to accept less than the amount owed on the balance of the mortgage.

It is called discounting the note! Many times there are accounting reasons that a bank would prefer to sell a discounted note rather than accepting a short pay-off of the mortgage. The results are essentially the same but for the bank, the accounting is quite different.

Example: Joe Smith owes $200,000 on the balance of his mortgage and is three months behind on payments. He has finally gotten back on his feet but the bank insists on getting all of the back payments in addition to the next months' payment or else they are going to foreclose. Joe is unable to meet these terms. You, as an investor, offer to buy the mortgage note from the bank, so they do not need to deal with this client in the future. The bank need not proceed with the very expensive and time consuming foreclosure process. You propose to purchase the existing note for $165,000. The value of the home is $250,000. The bank accepts your offer and you purchase the note.

As the new note holder, you negotiate with Joe to stay in the property and continue the same payments as before. The only difference is that he owes you $200,000 on a note that you purchased from the bank for $165,000. Discounted note transactions have the ability to produce guaranteed returns in the range of 12% - 30% and sometimes even more. Best of all, the investment is collateralized with the real property. In this example, if Joe defaults once again, you would foreclose and end up with a great rental property that has approximately $85,000 in equity.

As mentioned before, sellers often times will carry a private note in order to sell a property. After a short time, the note holder decides he/she would prefer to have cash instead of collecting small monthly payments. They offer to sell a good, performing note at a considerable discount. You recognize this could be a great opportunity for you to take a cash loan from your EIUL contract and fund the purchase of a discounted note. By the way, these notes can be available in amounts as little as $2,000 and as much as $500,000 or more. There is no limit to the possibilities!

"What if I am not a seasoned investor?" Learning how to find great real estate opportunities will be a part of the educational process. Your overall plan will require continuing education. It is not something you need to learn overnight. Remember, you learn how to crawl, walk and then run. In the meantime your EIUL contract continues to grow steadily and safely, and your family has protection with the additional benefit of insurance coverage. <u>A truly win-win situation!</u>

SUMMARY

You've heard all good things must come to an end! However, in your case this is just the beginning!

Let's fast forward a bit and review why the "Financial Wellness System™" works so well for individuals who have already attained financial success. From our past experience in the financial services industry, we find most wealthy individuals either worked hard to get where they are or they inherited their money. In either case, most of them seem to be especially concerned with wealth preservation and the reduction of taxes.

Without question, an Equity Indexed Universal Life contract is one of the best methods for transferring wealth to future generations. With good planning, it is also a great way to donate to a favorite charity. The Baby Boomer Generation will quickly be faced with this scenario and as we tell our clients, it is never too late to start a plan using an EIUL contract. The growth potential for a grandchild is phenomenal. There has never been a better method for creating wealth and establishing a banking system for the long-term for heirs of a large estate. We should add, it can be accomplished with minimal taxation and high returns.

No one's financial situation is the same. When we meet with a client, we completely analyze their entire portfolio. Only after careful consideration of the clients' needs and goals, are we able to make our recommendations. In your situation, your advisor will provide the same service for you.

There is a major financial crisis facing many families today. Unless they take full responsibility for their finances, they will continue through life with just enough money to get by and with little or no savings for retirement.

Prior to completing this book, an associate from the past, called me (Jerry) and asked to meet and discuss the subject of Lease/Option Contracts. He is a Realtor who has been in the business for 35 years. At our meeting, we determined it had been about 15 years since we last spoke to each other. A close friend of ours told him, I am an active investor in single family homes and well versed on the subject of Lease/Option Contracts. After reviewing his questions, we got into the subject of retirement. He told me, at his last birthday, he turned 60. Although he had a relatively successful career, he admitted he had no money saved for retirement. He told me, he simply never ever sat down and planned for his retirement.

As unfortunate as this might sound, there are many other people who are just like him. They simply never sat down and mapped out a plan. Recently, Raleigh and I talked to one of our clients who told us her mother is eighty two years old and still working. Fortunately, her mother is in good health. She needed to work because her Social Security income is insufficient to keep up with monthly expenses.

At Wealth2020, Inc., we stress the importance of principal protection. We are not saying that you should never venture into any type of risky investments or that you should not consider investing in your own business which might involve considerable risk. We are saying if you follow the proven "Financial Wellness System™" and apply the concepts to your individual circumstances, you will succeed. As your plan begins to develop and create the wealth you so richly deserve, more lucrative investment opportunities will present themselves to you. Without your base and foundation, they will only be ideas you could not act upon!

Financial planning is a serious subject and one that requires commitment and discipline. Learn the principles. They will work for you. At Wealth2020, Inc. we continually review new opportunities for our clients. We constantly meet with other industry professionals who have the best interest of our clients in mind. Never, at any time, do we profess to have all the answers. Successful people surround themselves with other successful people. It is all about assembling a team of like-minded professionals who want to help each other succeed. You need to do the same in your wealth building.

Many people have been instrumental in guiding our path. Successful people use these same concepts consistently. Many years of research, constant reading of books, analyzing markets and personal life experiences played an important role in helping us to formulate this book. We have designed a system that puts all the pieces of the prosperity puzzle together so they work best for you.

So, how do you get started? First, make sure that you fully understand the concepts and ideas. If you don't, go back and review the chapters which seem vague to you. From that point, you will need to sit down and determine exactly how you are going to fund your EIUL contract. Most importantly, you will need to determine approximately how much money you will need at the time of retirement. No matter how difficult it might seem to achieve your goal, don't let that be a deterrent. We find, once people establish their goals and put together a plan, many times they exceed their expectations. That is what makes this system so remarkable!

As we conclude, let us add at Wealth2020, Inc. we are always just a phone call or an E-mail away. It is our hope; we can be of assistance to you. We do not expect you to do this entirely by yourself.

We are always available to build a plan for you. The high yield investment returns are real and new opportunities are presented to us everyday. Our job is to sort them and to make sure there is small risk and if at all possible, a contractual guarantee of principal return.

Real Estate investment opportunities are safe and highly profitable. With guidance and knowledge you can succeed. Believe in yourself! Become knowledgeable! Take definitive action!

Continuous education should be one of your priorities. Unfortunately some people think once they get out of school their educational process is over. Today, more than ever, it is important you read and study as much information as possible to stay ahead of the game. Most schools teach only enough information to get a job. They rarely, if ever, teach how to make money work for you.

In the References/Acknowledgements, you will find a list of books we highly recommend. Read them as part of your continuing education.

This book introduces concepts which may be new to you. We end our book, but hopefully **begin a new chapter in the financial well being of your life**. Since this is <u>your</u> beginning, let's discuss one more very important concept.

<u>The power of time!</u> Time can be your friend or your enemy. From this day forward, the days, weeks, months and years will continue to go by whether you like it or not. Remember, the "Rule of 72" will tell you exactly how long it takes to double your money as it grows with various rates of return. The number of doubling periods is much greater, for a 25 year old person than it is for a 60 year old person. No matter how old you are, **<u>use the time wisely!</u>** Develop a plan and don't let <u>anyone</u> keep you from attaining your goals. **Especially you!**

Here is to your success!

Jerry Gallegos
Raleigh Makarechian

APPENDIX

- § Case Study – Actual Client Plan
- § The Johnson Family – The Rest of Their Story
- § Building Your Plan – A Guide for You
- § Summary of Services Offered

Case Study

John and Mary Smith

Wealth2020, Inc.

Presents

An Illustration
of a
Successful
Banking System

For

John and Mary Smith

Prepared By

Raleigh Makarechian and Jerry Gallegos

Wealth2020, Inc.
8156-E So. Wadsworth Boulevard, #155
Littleton, CO 80128

866-888-3636 Toll Free

info@wealth2020.com

or visit

www.Wealth2020.com

This is not a contract. The purpose of this plan is to illustrate the role of insurance in your affairs. All suggestions regarding taxes and other concerns should be reviewed with your personal counsel.

Financial Planning Summary
John and Mary Smith

Primary Objectives

- A retirement savings plan that will allow John and Mary Smith to quickly and safely amass wealth while assisting their children with college education. They look forward to preserving their current lifestyle in retirement.
- Put the idle equity in John and Mary Smith's primary residence to work for them.
- Create a banking system that will allow John and Mary Smith to finance their future Investments and help them build substantial wealth more quickly and safely.
- Reposition IRA savings to a self directed account that will provide safer investing opportunities.
- Increase tax deductions for John and Mary Smith.

Secondary Objectives

- Replace current income needs, as soon as feasible, with an alternate source of income whether passive or investment gains.
- Ensure that John's Family is protected in the event of Tony passing away unexpectedly. John understands that this is a side benefit of the plan, as we solved for the lowest possible Death Benefit.

Assumptions

- John's Date of Birth: 12/08/1957
- John does not smoke

Needs Overview – based upon our discussion

- John and Mary Smith are planning for retirement and are looking for a safe, reliable investment vehicle that does not need constant attention.
- Suggest:
  1) Based upon discussions with John, he would like to replace the family's current income in their retirement years. Looking forward, John has calculated a $55,000 to $60,000 annual cash flow need.
  2) Refinance primary residence to free up idle equity and reposition over time into an Equity Indexed Universal Life policy. This is projected to increase John and Mary Smith's tax deductions going forward.
  3) Reposition John and Mary Smith's IRA funds into a self-directed IRA to increase investment options available.

Current Savings Option

	Savings Type	Savings Current Balance	Savings Available Balance
John:	Checking	2,000	2,000
	Savings	1,000	1,000
	Stocks	30,000	30,000
	401K	90,000	0
	IRA	62,500	46,875
Mary:	401K	50,000	0
	IRA	62,500	46,875
	Home Equity	242,000	237,000
	Rental Equity	60,000	55,000
Subtotals:		$600,000	$418,750

Current Insurance Option

Insurance Type	Death Benefit	Name of Insured	Cash Value Age 65
Term	$100,000	John	N/A
Term	$50,000	Mary	N/A
Subtotal:	$150,000		

Proposed Insurance and Savings Option

Insurance Plan	Death Benefit	Annual Premium	Total Premiums Paid In	Cash Value Age 65
Equity Indexed Universal Life ***Insured:*** *John Smith*	$829,623	$50,000	$250,000	$651,397

Notes:

Tax Free Access prior to age 59 1/2. No 10% early withdrawal penalties as with a typical IRA.

Withdrawals/Loans for children's education will NOT reduce eligibility for college financial aid.

Material discussed in this summary is meant for general illustration and/or informational purposes only and is not to be construed as tax, legal, or investment advice. Although the information has been gathered from sources believed to be reliable, please note that individual situations can vary, therefore, the information should be relied upon when coordinated with individual professional advice.

Illustrations from John and Mary Smith's Plan (First Two Pages Only – Page 1):

Designed for: John H Smith
Issue Age: 49
Male, Standard Non-Tobacco

$829,623 Selected Face Amount
Initial Annual Premium: $50,000.00
Initial Death Benefit Option: Level

Supplemental Report Description: This report shows both the account value and cash surrender value, and lists the schedule of surrender charges for the illustrated policy.

							Non-Guaranteed Assumed			
End of Year	Age	Modal Premium	Times Per Year	Annual Premium	Cash From Policy	Annual Outlay	Surr Cash Value	Surr Charge	Account Value	Death Benefit
1	50	50,000	1	50,000	0	50,000	16,390	29,410	45,800	829,623
2	51	50,000	1	50,000	0	50,000	67,982	27,449	95,432	829,623
3	52	50,000	1	50,000	0	50,000	123,813	25,489	149,302	829,623
4	53	50,000	1	50,000	0	50,000	184,331	23,528	207,860	829,623
5	54	50,000	1	50,000	0	50,000	249,980	21,567	271,548	829,623
6	55	0	1	0	0	0	269,726	19,607	289,333	829,623
7	56	0	1	0	0	0	290,949	17,646	308,595	829,623
8	57	0	1	0	0	0	313,788	15,685	329,473	829,623
9	58	0	1	0	0	0	338,375	13,725	352,099	829,623
10	59	0	1	0	0	0	368,509	11,764	380,273	829,623
				250,000	0	250,000				
11	60	0	1	0	0	0	403,712	9,803	413,515	829,623
12	61	0	1	0	0	0	442,108	7,843	449,951	829,623
13	62	0	1	0	0	0	484,069	5,882	489,951	829,623
14	63	0	1	0	0	0	530,024	3,921	533,945	829,623
15	64	0	1	0	0	0	580,457	1,961	582,417	829,623
16	65	0	1	0	74,074	-74,074	555,975	0	635,198	750,400
17	66	0	1	0	74,074	-74,074	529,700	0	693,654	665,669
18	67	0	1	0	74,074	-74,074	503,609	0	758,184	640,082
19	68	0	1	0	74,074	-74,074	477,385	0	828,881	618,295
20	69	0	1	0	74,074	-74,074	451,170	0	906,325	596,182
				250,000	370,369	-120,369				
21	70	0	1	0	74,074	-74,074	425,136	0	991,156	573,810
22	71	0	1	0	74,074	-74,074	399,491	0	1,084,083	540,422
23	72	0	1	0	74,074	-74,074	374,728	0	1,186,135	505,202
24	73	0	1	0	74,074	-74,074	351,261	0	1,298,299	468,108
25	74	0	1	0	74,074	-74,074	329,595	0	1,421,694	429,114

The values and benefits are not guaranteed and are subject to change unless the column is marked guaranteed. This supplemental illustration must be accompanied by a basic illustration for required disclosure.

Illustrations from John and Mary Smith's Plan (Page 2):

Designed for: John H Smith
Issue Age: 49
Male, Standard Non-Tobacco

$829,623 Selected Face Amount
Initial Annual Premium: $50,000.00
Initial Death Benefit Option: Level

Supplemental Report Description: This report shows both the account value and cash surrender value, and lists the schedule of surrender charges for the illustrated policy.

							Non-Guaranteed Assumed			
End of Year	Age	Modal Premium	Times Per Year	Annual Premium	Cash From Policy	Annual Outlay	Surr Cash Value	Surr Charge	Account Value	Death Benefit
26	75	0	1	0	74,074	-74,074	310,346	0	1,557,589	388,226
27	76	0	1	0	74,074	-74,074	294,266	0	1,707,439	379,638
28	77	0	1	0	74,074	-74,074	281,060	0	1,871,698	374,645
29	78	0	1	0	74,074	-74,074	271,257	0	2,051,697	373,841
30	79	0	1	0	74,074	-74,074	265,444	0	2,248,882	377,888
				250,000	1,111,106	-861,106				
31	80	0	1	0	74,074	-74,074	264,273	0	2,464,820	387,514
32	81	0	1	0	74,074	-74,074	268,464	0	2,701,213	403,524
33	82	0	1	0	74,074	-74,074	278,808	0	2,959,902	426,803
34	83	0	1	0	74,074	-74,074	296,187	0	3,242,891	458,332
35	84	0	1	0	74,074	-74,074	321,565	0	3,552,343	499,182
36	85	0	1	0	74,074	-74,074	355,956	0	3,890,557	550,484
37	86	0	1	0	74,074	-74,074	400,460	0	4,260,005	613,461
38	87	0	1	0	74,074	-74,074	456,262	0	4,663,341	689,429
39	88	0	1	0	74,074	-74,074	524,635	0	5,103,407	779,805
40	89	0	1	0	74,074	-74,074	606,942	0	5,583,248	886,104
				250,000	1,851,843	-1,601,843				
41	90	0	1	0	74,074	-74,074	704,675	0	6,106,151	1,009,983
42	91	0	1	0	74,074	-74,074	819,469	0	6,675,672	1,086,496
43	92	0	1	0	74,074	-74,074	961,649	0	7,304,191	1,180,775
44	93	0	1	0	74,074	-74,074	1,136,879	0	7,999,570	1,296,871
45	94	0	1	0	74,074	-74,074	1,352,016	0	8,771,015	1,439,726
46	95	0	1	0	74,074	-74,074	1,615,352	0	9,629,333	1,615,352
47	96	0	1	0	74,074	-74,074	1,934,260	0	10,584,587	1,934,260
48	97	0	1	0	74,074	-74,074	2,303,956	0	11,634,865	2,303,956
49	98	0	1	0	74,074	-74,074	2,730,815	0	12,789,621	2,730,815
50	99	0	1	0	74,074	-74,074	3,221,943	0	14,059,247	3,221,943
				250,000	2,592,580	-2,342,580				

The values and benefits are not guaranteed and are subject to change unless the column is marked guaranteed. This supplemental illustration must be accompanied by a basic illustration for required disclosure.

As you can see from the illustration, John and Mary can look forward to a tax-free retirement income of $74,074 beginning at John's age 65 and continuing into perpetuity. A combination of Alternative Investments suggested between now and retirement will allow John and Mary to secure a bright retirement future.

The Johnson Family

The Rest of Their Story

The Rest of the Story

Early in our story, we discussed the Johnson family retirement plan. We showed you what they planned to do, before they became clients. If you will recall from pages 16 – 19, they planned to save $8,000 per year in a qualified retirement plan. Their vehicle of choice was a 401(k). **<u>Chart A</u>**, on page 18, showed us that if they made deposits of $8,000 per year annually for 30 years they would amass $1,188,602 in 401(k) savings. Then we showed you what the fate of their retirement plan would be, in the following chart.

Will the Johnson's Qualified Retirement Plan Survive?

Name: Mr. and Mrs. Johnson

Current Age: 35 Ret. Age: 65 Years Money to Grow: 30
Present Value of QRP: $8,000
Annual Contributions: $8,000 Rate of Inflation: 3.50%
Expected ROR 9.00% Years: 30
Inflation Rate: 3.50% Future Value Needed to Match: $202,089
Current Annual Income: $80,000 Present Value (Income after Contrib): $ 72,000
Contribution Tax Deductions - Estimated: $72,000 Heirs Marginal Tax Bracket: 30%
Est. Retirement Marginal Tax Bracket: 20%

After Tax Net Annual Income: $202,089 Start Withdraw At Age: 65

Year	Age	IRA Balance	IRA Withdraw	Taxes Paid	Net After Tax Withdraw	IRA Balance After Withdraw	Net to Heirs After Tax
1	65	$ 1,188,602	$ 252,611	$ 50,522	$ 202,089	$ 935,991	$ 655,193
2	66	$ 1,020,230	$ 252,611	$ 50,522	$ 202,089	$ 767,618	$ 537,333
3	67	$ 836,704	$ 252,611	$ 50,522	$ 202,089	$ 584,092	$ 408,865
4	68	$ 636,661	$ 252,611	$ 50,522	$ 202,089	$ 384,049	$ 268,835
5	69	$ 418,614	$ 252,611	$ 50,522	$ 202,089	$ 166,002	$ 116,202
6	70	$ 180,943	$ 180,943	$ 36,189	$ 144,754	$ -	$ -
7	71	$ -	$ -	$ -	$ -	$ -	$ -
8	72	$ -	$ -	$ -	$ -	$ -	$ -
9	73	$ -	$ -	$ -	$ -	$ -	$ -
10	74	$ -	$ -	$ -	$ -	$ -	$ -
11	75	$ -	$ -	$ -	$ -	$ -	$ -
12	76	$ -	$ -	$ -	$ -	$ -	$ -
13	77	$ -	$ -	$ -	$ -	$ -	$ -
14	78	$ -	$ -	$ -	$ -	$ -	$ -
		TOTALS:	$1,444,000	$ 288,800	$1,155,200		

Let's review what could have happened to the Johnson's if they had not changed course. Taking inflation into account, 30 years from now they will require $202,089 each year to maintain the same standard of living that they enjoy today. They will, however, be forced to withdraw a substantially larger amount ($252,111) to ensure that they can pay the taxes they owe each year. They pay $50,522 that first year and receive a net amount of $202,089 to live on. The Johnson's paid out $288,800 in taxes; while deductions on the contributions they made over that 30 year period were estimated to be $72,000. They paid back 4 times the amount of the benefit they received in the prior 30; only 6 years into retirement!

You may argue that they should just choose to live on a smaller amount of money each year. However, if they simply change the instrument in which they save their hard-earned dollars, you will see that they can have the best of both worlds.

They are spending little or no additional money out of pocket now but end up with a more secure retirement later.

Let us finish their story for you. When the Johnson's came to us, we showed them what an EIUL policy could do for them. Following is an illustration using the same $8,000 per year over 30 years. As you can see, in the illustration below (reference continuation on page 75), the Johnson's will be able to access their money on a tax-free basis beginning at 65. Each year, they can look forward to a $143,014 tax-free income. This is the equivalent of $178,767 in taxable income. They will enjoy $143,014 tax-free, annually. Remember, their original plan ran out in less than 6 years. With some additional planning, Wealth2020, Inc. can replace their entire income requirement into perpetuity.

One of the best aspects of this plan is that the Johnson's do not have a looming tax burden. They will effectively avoid paying **hundreds of thousands** in taxes during retirement.

Designed for: Johnson Family — $542,010 Selected Face Amount
Issue Age: 34 — Initial Annual Premium: $8,000.00
Male, Standard Non-Tobacco — Initial Death Benefit Option: Level

Supplemental Report Description: This report shows both the account value and cash surrender value, and lists the schedule of surrender charges for the illustrated policy.

							Non-Guaranteed Assumed			
End of Year	Age	Modal Premium	Times Per Year	Annual Premium	Cash From Policy	Annual Outlay	Surr Cash Value	Surr Charge	Account Value	Death Benefit
1	35	8,000	1	8,000	0	8,000	0	10,401	6,253	542,010
2	36	8,000	1	8,000	0	8,000	3,314	9,708	13,022	542,010
3	37	8,000	1	8,000	0	8,000	11,316	9,014	20,331	542,010
4	38	8,000	1	8,000	0	8,000	19,943	8,321	28,264	542,010
5	39	8,000	1	8,000	0	8,000	29,242	7,628	36,869	542,010
6	40	8,000	1	8,000	0	8,000	39,280	6,934	46,214	542,010
7	41	8,000	1	8,000	0	8,000	50,118	6,241	56,359	542,010
8	42	8,000	1	8,000	0	8,000	61,812	5,547	67,359	542,010
9	43	8,000	1	8,000	0	8,000	74,442	4,854	79,296	542,010
10	44	8,000	1	8,000	0	8,000	88,987	4,160	93,147	542,010
				80,000	0	80,000				
11	45	8,000	1	8,000	0	8,000	105,809	3,467	109,276	542,010
12	46	8,000	1	8,000	0	8,000	124,194	2,774	126,968	542,010
13	47	8,000	1	8,000	0	8,000	144,296	2,080	146,377	542,010
14	48	8,000	1	8,000	0	8,000	166,277	1,387	167,664	542,010
15	49	8,000	1	8,000	0	8,000	190,350	693	191,044	542,010
16	50	8,000	1	8,000	0	8,000	216,616	0	216,616	542,010
17	51	8,000	1	8,000	0	8,000	244,702	0	244,702	542,010
18	52	8,000	1	8,000	0	8,000	275,573	0	275,573	542,010
19	53	8,000	1	8,000	0	8,000	309,520	0	309,520	542,010
20	54	8,000	1	8,000	0	8,000	346,862	0	346,862	544,573
				160,000	0	160,000				
21	55	8,000	1	8,000	0	8,000	387,886	0	387,886	581,830
22	56	8,000	1	8,000	0	8,000	432,913	0	432,913	632,053
23	57	8,000	1	8,000	0	8,000	482,285	0	482,285	684,844
24	58	8,000	1	8,000	0	8,000	536,429	0	536,429	740,273
25	59	8,000	1	8,000	0	8,000	595,815	0	595,815	798,392

The values and benefits are not guaranteed and are subject to change unless the column is marked guaranteed. This supplemental illustration must be accompanied by a basic illustration for required disclosure.

Supplemental Report Description: This report shows both the account value and cash surrender value, and lists the schedule of surrender charges for the illustrated policy.

							Non-Guaranteed Assumed			
End of Year	Age	Modal Premium	Times Per Year	Annual Premium	Cash From Policy	Annual Outlay	Surr Cash Value	Surr Charge	Account Value	Death Benefit
26	60	8,000	1	8,000	0	8,000	660,964	0	660,964	859,253
27	61	8,000	1	8,000	0	8,000	732,458	0	732,458	937,546
28	62	8,000	1	8,000	0	8,000	810,819	0	810,819	1,021,632
29	63	8,000	1	8,000	0	8,000	896,710	0	896,710	1,111,921
30	64	8,000	1	8,000	0	8,000	990,869	0	990,869	1,208,861
				240,000	0	240,000				
31	65	0	1	0	0	0	1,086,070	0	1,086,070	1,303,284
32	66	0	1	0	143,014	-143,014	1,037,544	0	1,190,500	1,263,739
33	67	0	1	0	143,014	-143,014	988,371	0	1,304,916	1,223,255
34	68	0	1	0	143,014	-143,014	938,754	0	1,430,261	1,181,899
35	69	0	1	0	143,014	-143,014	888,940	0	1,567,572	1,139,752
36	70	0	1	0	143,014	-143,014	839,221	0	1,717,987	1,096,919
37	71	0	1	0	143,014	-143,014	789,946	0	1,882,758	1,034,704
38	72	0	1	0	143,014	-143,014	741,964	0	2,063,703	968,971
39	73	0	1	0	143,014	-143,014	695,989	0	2,262,570	899,621
40	74	0	1	0	143,014	-143,014	652,894	0	2,481,338	826,588
				240,000	1,287,125	-1,047,125				
41	75	0	1	0	143,014	-143,014	613,744	0	2,722,255	749,857
42	76	0	1	0	143,014	-143,014	579,846	0	2,987,894	729,240
43	77	0	1	0	143,014	-143,014	550,673	0	3,279,081	714,627
44	78	0	1	0	143,014	-143,014	527,137	0	3,598,177	707,046
45	79	0	1	0	143,014	-143,014	510,256	0	3,947,746	707,643
46	80	0	1	0	143,014	-143,014	501,153	0	4,330,570	717,682
47	81	0	1	0	143,014	-143,014	501,074	0	4,749,663	738,558
48	82	0	1	0	143,014	-143,014	511,393	0	5,208,294	771,808
49	83	0	1	0	143,014	-143,014	533,636	0	5,710,015	819,136
50	84	0	1	0	143,014	-143,014	569,472	0	6,258,663	882,405
				240,000	2,717,264	-2,477,264				

The values and benefits are not guaranteed and are subject to change unless the column is marked guaranteed. This supplemental illustration must be accompanied by a basic illustration for required disclosure.

Supplemental Report Description: This report shows both the account value and cash surrender value, and lists the schedule of surrender charges for the illustrated policy.

							Non-Guaranteed Assumed			
End of Year	Age	Modal Premium	Times Per Year	Annual Premium	Cash From Policy	Annual Outlay	Surr Cash Value	Surr Charge	Account Value	Death Benefit
51	85	0	1	0	143,014	-143,014	620,664	0	6,858,316	963,580
52	86	0	1	0	143,014	-143,014	689,118	0	7,513,360	1,064,786
53	87	0	1	0	143,014	-143,014	776,889	0	8,228,499	1,188,314
54	88	0	1	0	143,014	-143,014	886,186	0	9,008,778	1,336,624
55	89	0	1	0	143,014	-143,014	1,019,376	0	9,859,597	1,512,355
56	90	0	1	0	143,014	-143,014	1,179,047	0	10,786,785	1,718,386
57	91	0	1	0	143,014	-143,014	1,368,039	0	11,796,650	1,839,905
58	92	0	1	0	143,014	-143,014	1,604,547	0	12,911,098	1,991,880
59	93	0	1	0	143,014	-143,014	1,898,534	0	14,144,058	2,181,415
60	94	0	1	0	143,014	-143,014	2,262,070	0	15,511,844	2,417,189
				240,000	4,147,403	-3,907,403				
61	95	0	1	0	143,014	-143,014	2,709,768	0	17,033,605	2,709,768
62	96	0	1	0	143,014	-143,014	3,254,612	0	18,727,180	3,254,612
63	97	0	1	0	143,014	-143,014	3,888,068	0	20,589,224	3,888,068
64	98	0	1	0	143,014	-143,014	4,621,342	0	22,636,497	4,621,342
65	99	0	1	0	143,014	-143,014	5,466,922	0	24,887,424	5,466,922
66	100	0	1	0	143,014	-143,014	6,438,718	0	27,362,264	6,438,718
67	101	0	1	0	143,014	-143,014	7,552,210	0	30,083,291	7,552,210
68	102	0	1	0	143,014	-143,014	8,824,625	0	33,074,994	8,824,625
69	103	0	1	0	143,014	-143,014	10,275,120	0	36,364,299	10,275,120
70	104	0	1	0	143,014	-143,014	11,924,989	0	39,980,810	11,924,989
				240,000	5,577,541	-5,337,541				
71	105	0	1	0	143,014	-143,014	13,797,895	0	43,957,077	13,797,895
72	106	0	1	0	143,014	-143,014	15,920,120	0	48,328,885	15,920,120
73	107	0	1	0	143,014	-143,014	18,320,846	0	53,135,584	18,320,846
74	108	0	1	0	143,014	-143,014	21,032,463	0	58,420,432	21,032,463
75	109	0	1	0	143,014	-143,014	24,090,906	0	64,230,995	24,090,906
76	110	0	1	0	143,014	-143,014	27,536,036	0	70,619,568	27,536,036
				240,000	6,435,625	-6,195,625				

The values and benefits are not guaranteed and are subject to change unless the column is marked guaranteed. This supplemental illustration must be accompanied by a basic illustration for required disclosure.

Building <u>Your</u> Plan

A Guide for You

Building Your Plan

While it is possible to do your own planning, you may need the assistance of a Financial Planner who has a "Life License" to set up and maintain your life insurance contract. Your Equity Indexed Universal Life policy is your road-map to success and, as such, you want to begin with a solid foundation. More importantly, you want to be sure to stay on track.

At Wealth2020, Inc., you can consult with Jerry Gallegos or Raleigh Makarechian for assistance in setting up your individual Life Insurance contract.

Following are the steps you will need to ensure success in your retirement planning. It takes input from you and your planner.

1) The greatest portion of your planning will come from determining what your future budget will look like. Take a look at your annual cash flow requirements. This is the amount of money that you require to cover your living and entertainment expenses. Next, using this figure you will work 'backwards' to determine what actions you need to take today in establishing an Equity Indexed UL policy to achieve your goals; in whole or in part according to your preference.

2) Your next step will be to determine the amount of after-tax cash flow you will need to live during your retirement years. Take the number of years until retirement (Retirement Age minus your Current Age). Divide this number by the current inflation factor – let's assume 5%. Remember, the Rule of 72 helps you calculate how fast your money will double and it can also help reveal just how fast you have to double your money to maintain today's standard of living accounting for inflation. Next multiply your current after-tax cash flow needs by that value.

   For Example: According to the rate of inflation (we will use the 5% noted above), you need to double your money every 14.4 years (calculated as 72 divided by 5). Let's assume you just happen to be 14 years away from retirement and that you currently live, comfortably on an after-tax income of $50,000.00. With this in mind, you will need at least $100,000.00 per year ($50,000 X 2) in after-tax retirement income just to maintain your current standard of living.

   In order to achieve this with the Equity Indexed Life Insurance Policy alone, you will need to plan to invest $67,500 per year for 5 years. 5 Years is the shortest time frame in which you can fully fund your plan. This way you maximize cash growth and minimize your policy associated expense. See the partial illustration for Mr. Max Sample below.

Partial Illustration for Mr. Max Sample (Page 1):

Designed for: Max Sample	$1,119,991 Selected Face Amount
Issue Age: 49	Initial Annual Premium: $67,500.00
Male, Standard Non-Tobacco	Initial Death Benefit Option: Level

Supplemental Report Description: This report shows both the account value and cash surrender value, and lists the schedule of surrender charges for the illustrated policy.

							Non-Guaranteed Assumed			
End of Year	**Age**	**Modal Premium**	**Times Per Year**	**Annual Premium**	**Cash From Policy**	**Annual Outlay**	**Surr Cash Value**	**Surr Charge**	**Account Value**	**Death Benefit**
1	50	67,500	1	67,500	0	67,500	22,149	39,703	61,852	1,119,991
2	51	67,500	1	67,500	0	67,500	91,822	37,057	128,879	1,119,991
3	52	67,500	1	67,500	0	67,500	167,238	34,410	201,648	1,119,991
4	53	67,500	1	67,500	0	67,500	248,968	31,763	280,731	1,119,991
5	54	67,500	1	67,500	0	67,500	337,627	29,116	366,743	1,119,991
6	55	0	1	0	0	0	364,321	26,469	390,790	1,119,991
7	56	0	1	0	0	0	393,010	23,822	416,832	1,119,991
8	57	0	1	0	0	0	423,886	21,175	445,062	1,119,991
9	58	0	1	0	0	0	457,126	18,528	475,654	1,119,991
10	59	0	1	0	0	0	497,862	15,881	513,743	1,119,991
				337,500	0	337,500				
11	60	0	1	0	0	0	545,447	13,235	558,682	1,119,991
12	61	0	1	0	0	0	597,350	10,588	607,938	1,119,991
13	62	0	1	0	0	0	654,073	7,941	662,014	1,119,991
14	63	0	1	0	0	0	716,196	5,294	721,490	1,119,991
15	64	0	1	0	0	0	784,373	2,647	787,020	1,119,991
16	65	0	1	0	100,128	-100,128	751,292	0	858,381	1,012,902
17	66	0	1	0	100,128	-100,128	715,792	0	937,416	898,368
18	67	0	1	0	100,128	-100,128	680,530	0	1,024,650	864,967
19	68	0	1	0	100,128	-100,128	645,088	0	1,120,219	835,525
20	69	0	1	0	100,128	-100,128	609,658	0	1,224,909	805,643
				337,500	500,642	-163,142				
21	70	0	1	0	100,128	-100,128	574,474	0	1,339,586	775,412
22	71	0	1	0	100,128	-100,128	539,816	0	1,465,207	730,293
23	72	0	1	0	100,128	-100,128	506,350	0	1,603,162	682,697
24	73	0	1	0	100,128	-100,128	474,637	0	1,754,788	632,568
25	74	0	1	0	100,128	-100,128	445,361	0	1,921,595	579,872

The values and benefits are not guaranteed and are subject to change unless the column is marked guaranteed. This supplemental illustration must be accompanied by a basic illustration for required disclosure.

Partial Illustration for Mr. Max Sample (Page 2):

Designed for: Max Sample	$1,119,991 Selected Face Amount
Issue Age: 49	Initial Annual Premium: $67,500.00
Male, Standard Non-Tobacco	Initial Death Benefit Option: Level

Supplemental Report Description: This report shows both the account value and cash surrender value, and lists the schedule of surrender charges for the illustrated policy.

							Non-Guaranteed Assumed			
End of Year	Age	Modal Premium	Times Per Year	Annual Premium	Cash From Policy	Annual Outlay	Surr Cash Value	Surr Charge	Account Value	Death Benefit
26	75	0	1	0	100,128	-100,128	419,351	0	2,105,300	524,616
27	76	0	1	0	100,128	-100,128	397,627	0	2,307,870	513,020
28	77	0	1	0	100,128	-100,128	379,788	0	2,529,918	506,284
29	78	0	1	0	100,128	-100,128	366,550	0	2,773,244	505,212
30	79	0	1	0	100,128	-100,128	358,708	0	3,039,802	510,698
				337,500	1,501,927	-1,164,427				
31	80	0	1	0	100,128	-100,128	357,143	0	3,331,711	523,728
32	81	0	1	0	100,128	-100,128	362,825	0	3,651,271	545,388
33	82	0	1	0	100,128	-100,128	376,828	0	4,000,972	576,877
34	83	0	1	0	100,128	-100,128	400,343	0	4,383,521	619,519
35	84	0	1	0	100,128	-100,128	434,670	0	4,801,844	674,762
36	85	0	1	0	100,128	-100,128	481,185	0	5,259,048	744,137
37	86	0	1	0	100,128	-100,128	541,372	0	5,758,476	829,296
38	87	0	1	0	100,128	-100,128	616,833	0	6,303,712	932,019
39	88	0	1	0	100,128	-100,128	709,290	0	6,898,603	1,054,220
40	89	0	1	0	100,128	-100,128	820,586	0	7,547,261	1,197,949
				337,500	2,503,211	-2,165,711				
41	90	0	1	0	100,128	-100,128	952,737	0	8,254,132	1,365,444
42	91	0	1	0	100,128	-100,128	1,107,954	0	9,024,021	1,468,915
43	92	0	1	0	100,128	-100,128	1,300,195	0	9,873,666	1,596,405
44	93	0	1	0	100,128	-100,128	1,537,115	0	10,813,692	1,753,389
45	94	0	1	0	100,128	-100,128	1,827,985	0	11,856,547	1,946,550
46	95	0	1	0	100,128	-100,128	2,184,013	0	13,016,837	2,184,013
47	96	0	1	0	100,128	-100,128	2,615,169	0	14,308,166	2,615,169
48	97	0	1	0	100,128	-100,128	3,114,983	0	15,727,951	3,114,983
49	98	0	1	0	100,128	-100,128	3,692,076	0	17,288,971	3,692,076
50	99	0	1	0	100,128	-100,128	4,356,051	0	19,005,274	4,356,051
				337,500	3,504,496	-3,166,996				

The values and benefits are not guaranteed and are subject to change unless the column is marked guaranteed. This supplemental illustration must be accompanied by a basic illustration for required disclosure.

3) Next, you will compile the following:

a) Bank Statements: Checking
Savings
IRA
401(k)

b) Determine the Amount of equity in your home

4) Total the values from all of the categories noted in Step 3 to determine your current liquid cash available for investing.

IRA funds: You will pay tax at your ordinary income rate and be assessed a pre-age 59 ½, 10% penalty (where applicable). This will allow you to project what your liquid cash is available from these sources.

401(k) funds: These may or may not be available to you. Depending upon your company's Vesting Schedule, some of the funds may be available to you. Check with your plan administrator to see if you will be able to take funds out for repositioning to your Life Insurance contract. You will pay tax at your ordinary income rate and may be assessed a pre-age 59 ½, 10% penalty here as well.

Despite the 10% penalty noted above, many of our clients pay this very willingly when they see what their funds can do for them when positioned for growth in the Equity Indexed UL policy. Refer to the "Will Your Qualified Retirement Plan Survive?" illustration for a review of the devastating effects taxes can have upon your wealth if you wait until your retirement years to pay them. We suggest that you pay them now and get started down the right path to amassing wealth.

5) Multiply your current liquid cash reserves (including home equity) by 25% (.25 X Total from 3) and 4), above). Why 25%? We don't want your Retirement Planning to bring your current lifestyle to a halt. We want to ensure that you enjoy the same (or better!) lifestyle in retirement as you do today and vice versa. Of course, we have clients who wish to reposition <u>considerably more</u> than 25% of their portfolio into the Equity Indexed Universal Life policy, because they see the power of tax-free compounding of funds. You may decide to reposition more or less depending upon how you want to proceed with the plan. The decision is ultimately yours.

6) Take the value from 5), above, and divide by the number of years over which you would like to fund your plan.

   a) If you decide to Superfund the policy, divide by 5.
   b) If you decide to fund the policy over 10 years divide by 10, of course.
   c) If you would like to capitalize the policy **and** Superfund the policy, add the amount of the monthly payment you will make to the result you calculated in 6) a, above. (Be sure to multiply your monthly payment by 12 before adding it to the amount in 6) to determine your total <u>annual</u> investment.)

7) Contact Jerry Gallegos or Raleigh Makarechian to assist you with setting up your Life Insurance policy, if necessary. Otherwise, you may proceed on your own as noted earlier.

8) Make arrangements with your Mortgage Broker or Bank for a home equity loan or to refinance your property entirely. This is the easiest way to Superfund your policy and the way the majority of our clients, decide to proceed with preparing for a successful retirement.

9) If you have elected to work with us, you should plan to meet with us (Jerry and Raleigh) on a consistent basis to review potential investment opportunities that will supercharge your wealth building process. Just a few investments over the life of your planning will have a dramatic impact on the wealth you amass. Our intention is to guide you in several each year.

10) Review your plan annually to ensure that you are keeping pace with your investment goals.

> ***Important note***: *Customarily, we advise that a client plan to draw on several sources for retirement income. Perhaps 50% or more of the retirement funds may come from the policy, with the remainder coming from Real Estate Investments – short and long-term. We will advise you how to safely achieve your goals.*

Wealth2020, Inc.

Summary of Services

One of the most important endeavors of any business is the development a network of successful professional contacts. This network will ultimately be the most valuable asset and will be the primary determining factor in that company's success. The financial services profession is no exception.

Once a client decides to incorporate our strategy into building their short and long-term wealth creation plan, we recognize that this is only the beginning. Professional relationships become a necessary component of achieving financial goals. At Wealth2020, Inc., we continually expand our network of professional contacts. You too, will discover that developing your core team will accelerate the growth of your financial plan.

Our number one objective is to assist our clients in anyway possible to reach their goals. One of the most gratifying aspects of working with our clients is observing the positive results they achieve.

Wealth2020, Inc. is dedicated to excellence! It has taken many years of research, trial and error and due diligence to develop a core team of like-minded professionals who enjoy working with us to ensure our clients succeed.

If you would like to benefit from our past years of experiences, we invite you to utilize our services in the future. We are only a phone call or E-mail away. The next two, five and ten years are going to produce astounding results for those who decide to join us and participate in their future success.

Our entire network is structured to provide the following services:

- Review and build a plan to serve as a financial foundation
- Continual market research of the highest quality EIUL products available
- Locate and recommend investment grade properties on a nation-wide basis
- Ensure asset class diversification according to risk profile for the short and long-term
- Locate safe, high yield business ventures
- Conduct annual plan reviews

"Nothing can be created without a cause."....(unknown)
Be your own cause and create your wealth!

Glossary

Arbitrage – Can be described as the difference between the investment rate of return and the rate at which funds are borrowed. (Investment ROR minus Borrowed Funds Rate = Arbitrage Rate of Return). Any time you can create arbitrage, you create a situation whereby the same dollar works twice for you.

Baby Boomer Generation - A group of people who were born during the period of increased birth rates when economic prosperity rose in many countries following World War II.

Cash flow – The minimum amount of cash needed to cover all costs associated with maintaining living expenses; a budget. Investors commonly refer to cash flow needs as a minimum amount of funds that must be paid out in order to maintain an investment in good standing.

Corruption - Dishonesty for personal gain: dishonest exploitation of power for personal gain.

CPI - The Consumer Price Index (CPI) is a measure of the average change over time in the prices paid by urban consumers for a market basket of consumer goods and services.

Debt - Something owed - an amount of money, a service, or an item of property that is owed to someone.

Demographics – Are characteristics and statistics of human population: the characteristics of a human population or part of it, especially its size, growth, density, distribution, and statistics regarding birth, marriage, disease, and death

Discretionary Income - These are the dollars in excess of monthly cash flow needs that are available to spend on any goods and services over and above what is required to maintain one's standard of living. Often-times consumers will spend discretionary income on luxury goods, travel or dining out.

Dow 30 – The Dow Jones Industrial Average (DJIA) is comprised of 30 stocks at any given time since its inception in1928.

DJIA – The Dow 30 – The Dow Jones Industrial Average is comprised of 30 stocks at any given time since its inception in1928.

Home Equity – The difference between the Market Value of any given home and the Mortgage Balanced Owed on that home.

Equity Indexed Universal Life Insurance – A life insurance contract designed for cash value accumulation.

Financial Freedom – When the amount of income you derive from passive investment activity exceeds your cash flow requirements on a monthly basis.

Financial Plan – Is the foundation to your savings and retirement planning success. Your financial plan lays the groundwork for the type of investing necessary to ensure savings success. A financial plan is very unique to each individual or family. It is important to monitor your progress relative to the plan from time to time.

Great American Dream – This concept entails the following: going to college, followed by getting a good job, then buying a house, paying off the mortgage on that house as soon as possible, and, finally, saving a little each month to ensure ultimate financial security in one's retirement years. This is a concept that worked well for our parents and grandparents given the times and circumstances in which they were applying the concepts. This is an outmoded way of conducting one's financial planning in today's world.

Great Depression – Was a global depression of the 1930s; a drastic decline in the world economy resulting in mass unemployment and widespread poverty that lasted from 1929 until 1939

High Yield Investments – The rate of return produced by these investments exceeds the true rate of inflation. Investing in high yield instruments allows one to amass wealth quickly.

Inflation – Inflation has been defined as a process of continuously rising prices, or equivalently, of a continuously falling value of money.

Information Technology - The use of technologies from computing, electronics, and telecommunications to process and distribute information in digital and other forms

Institutional Investor – Is an organization that invests: a financial institution such as an insurance company or pension fund that invests in securities, rather than an individual investor.

Low Yield Investments – These investments produce a rate of return that does not keep pace with the true rate of inflation. These products are typically referred to as retail investments and they are Certificates of Deposit, Mutual Funds, and Money Market accounts.

Market Value - Amount expected from open-market sale: the amount that a seller could expect to obtain for property or goods sold on the open market.

Mortgage Balance – The remaining balanced owed to the financial institution or bank through which you have obtained financing for your primary residence or an investment property.

New Global Economy - Globalization is the increasing interdependence, integration and interaction among people and corporations in disparate locations around the world. It is an umbrella term which refers to a complex of economic, trade, social, technological, cultural and political interrelationships. The term has been used as early as 1944, however Theodore Levitt is usually credited with its first use in an economic context.

Passive Investment – Income producing investment activities that require little or no effort on the part of the investor to ensure a successful outcome.

Procrastination – The act of putting off taking action until a later time. Don't procrastinate; take action today!

Rate of Return – This term is used to describe the amount of income generated by investment. This is the amount of income generated in a year by capital invested, expressed as a percentage of the total sum invested.

Retail Investor – A term used to describe the average investor or the last level of investor to receive a benefit from trading investment dollars for any particular investment product.

Retail Investments – A term used to describe mainstream investments available to Retail Investors. Certificates of Deposit (CDs), Mutual Funds, Money Market accounts are typical Retail Level Investments. Rates of return associated with these products barely keep pace with inflation.

Spend-able Income – Also known as *discretionary income*, is any income left over after paying necessary expenditures such as cost of living expenses each month.

Taxes - Money paid to government: an amount of money levied by a government on its citizens and used to run the government, the country, a state, a county, or a municipality.

Vesting Schedule – In reference to 401(k) plans, a vesting schedule is a schedule that sets forth the pace at which an employee may claim 100% of an employer's contributions to that 401(k) plan. A typical vesting plan may allow for an employee to vest at the rate of 20% per year. This would be referred to as a 5 year vesting schedule. After 5 years the employee is said to be 'fully vested' in his/her 401(k) plan.

Wealth – The definition of wealth can be very different for everyone.

> The Encarta definition is: 1) state of having much money: the state of having plenty of money or possessions.
>
> The Authors' definition is: a state of abundance and balance in all areas of life to include all of the following: physical health, abundance of possessions, abundance of monetary wealth, spirituality and healthy relationships.

Wealth Destroyers – There are four wealth destroyers that each of us are confronted with in our planning for retirement. Taxes - Debt - Inflation – Procrastination; Each one is defined here in the glossary for your convenience.

References

"401(k) Contributions" *http://beginnersinvest.about.com/od/401(k)/a/aa122104a_4.htm*

"Baby Boomer." *http://en.wikipedia.org/wiki/Baby_boomer*

http://www.bankrate.com *"Guard Your Portfolio Against Inflation"*

http://www.billsaver.com/household.html

http://www.BoomerProject.com

Bubble After Bubble in the Ongoing Bubble Boom, by Harry S. Dent, Jr.

"Corruption." *Microsoft Encarta*

"Debt." *Microsoft Encarta*

"Demographics." *Microsoft Encarta*

http://www.denverpost.com/economy/ci_5035160 , core rate of inflation inclusions/exclusions

http://www.federalreserve.gov

"Great Depression." *Microsoft Encarta*

How the Affluent Manage Home Equity to Safely and Conservatively Build Wealth, *author Steven Marshall*

"Inflation." *http://www.bls.gov/cpi/*

http://www.jasmts.com *The Shepherd Investment Strategist*

Middle class living on the edge?, by Debora Vrana
http://articles.moneycentral.msn.com/SavingandDebt/SaveMoney/MiddleClassLivingOnTheEdge.aspx

"Missed Fortune 101", by Douglas Andrew

"Nothing else in the world - not all the armies - is so powerful as an idea whose time has come."
– Victor Hugo *http://www.yuni.com/quotes/hugo.html*

"Rich Dad's Prophecy", by Robert T. Kiyosaki

"Rich Dad/Poor Dad", by Robert T. Kiyosaki

http://www.stock-market-crash.net/nikkei.htm

http://www.Stockcharts.com , Dow Chart 1900-Present

Harry S. Dent, Jr., "The Next Great Bubble Boom"

"The New Rules of Money", by Ric Edelman

The Unfortunate Facts of Life. *"The US Bureau of Labor and Statistics"*

"You Can Choose To Be Rich", by Robert Kiyosaki

"**31 Days to Profits in Probate Real Estate**", by Ron Mead the Probate Guy)

2007 401(k) Maximum Contribution Limits, Calculator *(By: Andy Boylan, Published: November 1, 2006)*

"Nothing will ever be attempted if all possible objections must first be overcome."

- Samuel Johnson

"We are all inventors, each sailing out on a voyage of discovery, guided each by a private chart, of which there is no duplicate. The world is all gates, all opportunities."

- Ralph Waldo Emerson

"Go confidently in the direction of your dreams!
Live the life you've imagined."

- Henry David Thoreau

www.ingramcontent.com/pod-product-compliance
Ingram Content Group UK Ltd.
Pitfield, Milton Keynes, MK11 3LW, UK
UKHW051508290926
15471UKWH00008B/1488